Bryan Foster

Love
is the
Meaning
of Life

Bryan Foster

Love

is the

Meaning

of Life

(2nd ed.)

(Author Articles)

Bryan Foster

GREAT
DEVELOPMENTS

Publishers

Bryan Foster

Published in 2022
Great Developments Publishers
Gold Coast, Queensland, Australia 4217
ABN: 13133435168 USA-EIN: 98-0689457

Creator: Foster, Bryan, 1957- author

Title: Love is the Meaning of Life (2nd ed) (Author Articles)

ISBN: (hardback)   9780645222005
ISBN: (large print paperback) 9780648952091
ISBN: (paperback)   9780645222012
ISBN: (ebook)   9780648952084

Love is the Meaning of Life (2nd ed)

Notes: Includes bibliographical references and index.

Websites will develop more detail on the *'GOD Today' Series* and similar themes over the next few years.

https://www.GodTodaySeries.com/
https://www.BryanFosterAuthor.com/
(20+) God Today | Facebook (Public site)

+ various other social media webpages being developed.

Developing:

https://www.JesusAndMahomadAreGod.com/
https://www.LoveIsTheMeaningOfLife.com/

Cover images: Bryan and Karen Foster (Great Developments Publishers), Gold Coast, Australia.
Cover photo: Bryan Foster
Photographic assistance: Andrew Foster (Austographer.com), British Columbia, Canada.
Graphics: Bryan Foster and Bookpod

DEDICATION

I dedicate this Book 8 in the *'GOD Today' Series* to my family.
To Karen, the love of my life, my wife of 43 years.
My rock, my Uluru, my Angel, my heart of Australia.
And to my children Leigh-Maree, Andrew and Jacqui,
daughter-in-law Shannon, grandchildren Kyan, Cruze, Felicity
and Ellie.
To my parents, Frank (dec. 2018) and Mary.
And to my siblings John, Sooz, and Clare and all my extended
family.
Thank you for all your love, support, and encouragement.
To my dear friends and colleagues, thank you so much.

CONTENTS

Book 8 (8A plus 8B Selections)

8A = *Love is the Meaning of Life*
         (The theme of this book.)

8B = *Love is the Meaning of Life:*
       God's Love
       (Selections from Book 6, if interested)

Bryan Foster

Book 8A
Love is the Meaning of Life

What is Love?

Love's Challenges

Bryan Foster

Love's Solutions

General Solutions

Gender Solutions

A Nation's First People's Solutions

Love is the Meaning of Life

Bryan Foster

Book 8B - Selections & Author Articles from Book 6

Book 6 = *Love is the Meaning of Life: God's Love (1st ed)*

Love is the Meaning of Life (2nd ed)

Discerned Truths by the Author from God

Content Tables for Books 1-7 in this *Series*

Bryan Foster

Books 8A and (8B = Selections & Author Articles from Book 6)

Foreword by Karen Foster

Bryan has been incredibly open to discussing his views on the critical topic of this book and the Series - LOVE - Book 8 - *Love is the Meaning of Life (2nd ed)*, 2022. This also covers having God as part of the discussion for many people, for in their beliefs, God is Love. However, the author will take another tact with Book 8. Bryan shows absolute respect for all people and all their different views on Love, God, evil and relationships. The way he approached this book was quite interesting for me and hopefully for you, too, primarily through its writing and the highlights in the writings. You are invited to explore fascinatingly affirming messages about Love for today.

If the reader desires, Book 8 in Bryan's latest *Series* continues discovering the Love that began with Books 1 and 3. Photobooks, Books 2 and 4, add to the exploration shown by the author in spectacular photographic images. Some images in Book 4 are almost impossible to believe and are inspiring and Truthful!

Bryan renews and continues exploring Love for all people. As an aside, for those interested, investigations show how God/Creator/All-Powerful, etc., can be followed by anyone wanting to explore such otherworldly powers. This builds on the appreciation of who God is, which began in his first book, and could inspire your life and faith story, as it did for Bryan. On a broader scale, each of the books in this *Series* invites you to join in the discovery of LOVE. This LOVE is potent and significantly impacts people.

(Karen and Bryan - married for 43 years.)

Preface

Love is the Meaning of Life (2nd ed), 2022

In the next book, *Love is the Meaning of Life (2nd ed)*, I will attempt what I consider to be an exciting, yet quite challenging writing approach. The initial plan was to have this book separate from the new *'GOD Today' Series* of nine books by 2022 and to have only minimal references to God, religion, or spirituality – in line with much of the secular world's approaches.

This Book 8A, *Love is the Meaning of Life (2nd ed)* is about 2/3 of this book's physical length and is the actual Book 8 for publication. Book 8B is about the final 1/3. Book 8B discusses considerable religious and spiritual points about God based on Book 6 of 9 in this *Series*. 8B is considered the religious version of Book 8. It emphasises the place of God in Love and that God=Absolute Love. This Book 8 has minimal religious, spiritual, and God inclusions. Yet, enough content to possibly challenge the secular followers' beliefs, especially about God. But it isn't overpowering to any degree, just present to assist those with interest.

I want to highlight that in my mind, true Love is something almost everyone on Earth strongly desires, both for themselves and others. For a large proportion of the population, Love is seen as the Meaning for their Lives. For others, LOVE may be all over the place and quite confusing. Some people have been so neglected and not given any real love over their lifetimes that they legitimately have not seriously experienced true LOVE. LOVE for these people may be a distant thought and experience, whether real or false. It may even be quite painful to relate to for some because of the harm, abuse, and neglect they received from a young age or some other period within their lives. Yet, we can all help these people discover Love and everything Love offers us if we are willing to help others.

But I realised during the writing of this Book 8 that for people to make informed, conscious decisions on this major belief about a God or no God, there had to be some well-respected views and opinions from the believers in God discussed also. These supported the reality of God and God's place within creation. Hence some have been included. Most are in Book 8B at the back, while the others are scattered throughout this Book 8A in the front section of this book you're reading. The minimal inclusions relating to God and Love are in the positions deliberately chosen for those who aren't that interested in the connection of God with Love. For any reader who doesn't want much of this *'God Today' Series* content, it is suggested they skim the 8B articles/sections in the back section of this book to find any relevant themes and then continue evaluating these or just leave those pages alone, maybe to come back to later.

No one is being ridiculed or questioned explicitly because of their different stances and beliefs. The typical variety of views, secular and religious/spiritual, will be considered in this latest book in this *Series*.

Therefore, for the secular, non-God believers or followers, I have included some beliefs from Book 6, which provides for God's place in this world for believers of God. This is not trying to change the reader's views and feelings - however, these thoughts from the faithful need to be included for a more complete discussion on this topic, as just mentioned. There is a balanced set of beliefs from the continuum, starting from absolute God to ending with absolute evil, to assist with your decision making.

I am approaching the reader of Book 8 as someone who is not too interested or not interested in God and God's relationship with creation and with them. The reader may believe in far greater powers than we have on Earth or be a total non-believer and rejector of God, an atheist. Or maybe someone between the extreme positions mentioned above on that continuum – i.e., between Absolute LOVE and Hate.

For those desiring a book with numerous references to God, the spiritual world and Love, you would be best reading the 1st edition of this book, Book 6 in this *'GOD Today' Series - Love is the Meaning of Life: GOD's Love* (1st ed), 2021.

The number one reason for living and existing is often private for strongly secular believers. They believe only (sometimes mostly) in their chosen ways, along with others who have these same or similar beliefs. No higher force is needed for these people. And, for many of these them, seeing any benefit in a heavenly power is a sign of personal weakness. Many believe that needing a god is weak. Why? Because many strongly believe in individual choices and that other human loving relationships are all you need. If these people are not harming anyone or being harmed by others, in most cases, they think they live good, wholesome lives and do not need any other outside influences. I can accept these views as being strongly appropriate for many people because these are so common among non-God, secular believers in our western, first world. Many people believe this is correct when viewing that God and religions do evil or wrongdoings! God cannot do evil because that is opposite to what God IS, Absolute Love. People deliberately or accidentally do evil due to their Free Choice, which causes harm and pain to others and themselves.

However, here comes the challenge I am now facing. Love gives us powerful meaning and support for our lives. I will explore Love from various non-religious, non-Godly angles, looking at both the positives and the challenges to Love occurring within our world and in loving relationships. I link Love to God in a non-threatening way. At least as an introduction to this possibility of a divine Creator for those readers. No forced beliefs here! But to offer a gentle challenge, of there being one absolutely loving God for eternity for everyone and every religion - who adds so much to the Love story and the human needs for Love. Followers of God and Love are not weak. They are powerful.

You are strongly invited to be open in your search for Love and its meaning in life. I ask you to be prepared to consider the genuine arguments for both a divine presence and for a non-godly existence. Don't throw the book away just because of a challenge to your beliefs, developing or firmly held. One reason for you to read this book may be that you find a few or many points to your liking, which may genuinely bring you closer to an existence you may never have thought of or were never going to consider seriously, for various reasons. Start by talking to and listening for God (i.e., prayer, but use multiple methods from 'free style' to highly organised liturgical Church-style prayer). Then try discussions and explorations with friends, colleagues, religious people, etc. There is definitely no need to attack the listener you choose or for them to attack you. Be genuinely open-minded and give each other space and time to tease out the challenges and questions.

Introduction

What is true Love? Where does it come from? How do we experience it? Is there, Absolute Love? What is Absolute Love, if so? Is there anything needed for me to have true Love? Can other entities or forces depth our Love for each other? What about those who only believe in the physical world? Does this affect their depth of Love?

Where does Love come from? Can we all have it?

We have the freedom to decide to be loving or otherwise. These last two books in this *Series*, Book 8 - *Love is the Meaning of Life (2nd ed)* and Book 9 - *Love is the Meaning of Life Photobook Companion,* aim to assist the readers with their search for true Love and what place other people play in their lives.

How does Love work independently of higher powers if these powers exist? Having that unlimited support and guidance from others within our communities allows our Love for others and their Love for us to be 'depthed' significantly. Sometimes this may even be otherworldly - to be at an unexpected depth of engagement with each of us, at some very interesting times during our lives.

Love is the Meaning of Life (2nd ed) is the next book in Bryan Foster's latest *Series*. The first book in the *Series* highlighted twenty-six examples from the author's life, showing examples of where Love played a significant place for Bryan and others. Each story also contains examples of what appeared to be outside sources, impacting on those affected. Often there were subtly inspired messages or directions to take. Love was an integral aspect of all these stories. Sharing our genuine Love stories helps us all depth our appreciation of Love and how this Love is central to our genuine happiness within ourselves and each other. What similar sorts of stories do you, the reader, have? How have you found love in today's world, and how have you used it to better yourself and others?

The primary and essential question introduces this book: What is Love? This question will be explored primarily from the secular world's stance in this second edition book, with a few gentle challenges of spiritual viewpoints included. As he expects so do most people, the author believes that it would be a disservice for people not to read other views about Love and its historical and present reality within various cultures in our world.

There are so many aspects and features of Love that are needed to be explored in considerable depth to gain a proper appreciation of Love and how it affects us individually. These will be placed within various themes and experiences of the author and others. Each is a down-to-Earth exploration and finding. Each is real and will have a different reaction for readers according to their own experiences.

Once this is explored, then the challenges to Love are discussed. In most situations, people could improve their relations with others, whether in outright loving relationships or as one of a myriad of levels of loving relations. Various suggestions are offered to help us maintain our loving relationships, no matter their depth to each person concerned.

We next consider how people believe that spiritual forces may impact our relationships, whether we are aware of this impact or not. Readers are invited to join this journey to appreciate or acknowledge the possibility of faith in the Creator of the universe/the all-powerful in loving relationships. Once again, the challenges to this belief and various solutions to the difficulties are explored.

Love is both a most difficult concept to appreciate and a most rewarding and life-enhancing strengthening of what it is to be fully and utterly human in Love with others and the various fauna and flora in our living environments.

A depth of understanding and appreciation of Love explains how Love is integral and necessary for each of our lives. Love brings joy, happiness, forgiveness, empathy, etc., to relationships. People typically fear violence or various forms of abuse or other evil dispositions, which could become a part of their relationships, especially in their key relationships. In that case, these are not loving relationships. These abusive behaviours are evil!

Love is also an aspect of the natural world of fauna and flora. People often feel contentment when surrounded by pets, animals, and flora. That special place nearby or even our backyard or local park become places of solace and positive life-forces. We are all invited to be open to such incredible Life experiences on Earth.

Love is the foundation of life! It is literally the Meaning of Life for this author and many other readers and believers worldwide! I believe that many readers would agree. It is what gives life an incredible depth. It is from Love that all our endeavours, problem-solving, and successes will be managed. Wherever we are on the Love continuum will impact the choices we make. Love is/should be central to these choices.

Do you believe that the religiously faithful believers' wisdom sees that God leads us wholeheartedly with Absolute, Divine Love? It is a most freeing, exhilarating, and emotional response for believers. God only gives Good and never evil. *People who choose evil choices must accept the outcomes of their decisions.* Yet, God still has a mystery about much of this belief. After all, 'He' is the greatest mystery to all people, believers and non-believers alike. God is relatively unknown by many or maybe too complicated or mysterious for others. Yet, gently working with and through people for them to better appreciate the Divine, the Absolute Love, and the saviour of all becomes a human necessity within this Loving world. We feel the Love.

Are we on our own personal adventures of life? Are we aware of when these Loving situations arise for us? Are we authentically open to these experiences of Love (and maybe a 'celestial power' for the believers) and often life-changing adventures? Life can take various and exciting pathways. We have choices and need to be ready for when these come our way.

Most faithful believers in God, and some non-believers in God, believe that all people will have the opportunity to decide whether to reach that ultimate LOVE with and for the Absolute Good (for believers, this happens to be God) at our last moments of life or first moments of death. More than likely, this will be all people's final decision at their moment of death – to choose the all-powerful Creator of everything or to choose evil? Do the secularists see any future after death? Or does everything just abruptly stop for them? *Everyone will have their last chance at death to choose God or Evil. This will depend so much on our earthly lifestyle and beliefs – Love or Evil are the last options from which we choose.*

Once we open ourselves up to LOVE and let go of the negativity or disbelief surrounding us and how we often feel in our world today, we will experience more LOVE deeply and inherently.

Opening up means allowing various thoughts from any background source, etc., to reach us and will enable us to contemplate and decide upon the legitimacy of it.

We will grow into our LOVING LIFE journey with just that, LOVE. As humans, we should feel being called to something vastly different from our daily earthly experiences. It often feels like the best thing to search for when LOVE seems to be supported by something Immensely LOVING, but something we can't quite understand.

Some people, who are seriously challenged by either the belief in God or Evil or, in fact, anything beyond their control, will still be able to decide on either God or Evil at their death. *(Yet, there is no free ticket to Heaven for anyone!)* Could I suggest that those who may be don't want anything to do with God at this final, personal decision stage or elsewhere before Heaven or Hell could, for arguments' sake, take the opportunity to reflect upon the options available? This could encourage a swap of the two keywords - GOD with LOVE. (This is a genuine change purely because there is a strong belief in our world that God is Absolute Love.)

Making this an authentic decision, the interchanging of these two keywords allows the non-believers to ascertain their beliefs of Love with that word, Love! Their appreciation of what happens at death through Love will possibly be as for those who know and believe in God if there is no rejection of God once God is known about. *Rejecting the known God is evil! If this is the decision, the result is Hell for those decision-makers.* The secularists may like to do this swap anywhere within this book or in any other books in this Series. *This new perspective may open the chance to discover God, even though this wasn't the original intention.*

We are forever being called to LOVE by so many people worldwide –for believers in God; this may also include a calling for us back home with the Creator - well beyond the physical world. This is how our salvation in Heaven develops. Can we accept God? This absolutely Loving God. Love thoroughly, as God loves each of us equally and Absolutely LOVINGLY! Regular prayer, helping others in need, looking after ourselves, etc., is essential for LOVE's excellent, honest quality and directions offered! This is, therefore, a significant challenge for most secularists. And, for many non-secularists, those faithful believers in God.

For those open-minded or at least somewhat interested, will in time, with the constant searching and acknowledgement of God and God's magnificence and awesomeness, and our constant calling on Love or God to assist us with our lives, relationships, and human needs, *we will initially become one with God while on Earth. Life in Heaven begins through our Love of God and acknowledging God's Absolute Love for all people equally while living on this Earth.* Only after our death will we be offered complete Absolute LOVE beyond anything we could ever imagine in Heaven with all those from back to the Creation time.

Only the genuinely evil, haters and rejectors of a God they know of or about at their death will be permanently in Hell's solitude, loneliness, and hateful existence forever, through their personal decision of the choice of evil. *An honest secular, non-believer, who doesn't reject God but just doesn't really know God, can at the end of their lives choose God and not evil, at death.*

It is worth exploring this option for secularists and non-believers. Can non-believers also go to Heaven? YES. It is commonly believed that almost everyone (but not everyone literally) goes to Heaven, eventually. Those who end up in the other 'permanent destination' after death end permanently in Hell. Heaven is not an option for those who REJECT GOD outright! Those who know of or about GOD but continually choose evil ways, opposite to GOD's ways, exist in a sinful, non-loving world of their making, while still on Earth, which would generally continue this way after their death if they cannot change their practices and beliefs towards God while on Earth or at that moment of death.

It is felt that it has been commonly discerned that everyone will have one last final choice on their at-death destination at or immediately after death. Those who don't know or believe in God but don't reject God, who generally lived good, wholesome, loving lives, will most likely choose Heaven. This loving existence is what they appreciated more than anything else while alive. Therefore, non-believers can end up in perfect presence with the Creator and all other loving souls – if this is God's choice for them once they have decided their own choice – Absolute Love/God or Evil. This is the final time for an authentic, genuine decision by each person made individually before and with God! The personal rejection of the known God causes the decision to end up in the Evil, non-God, finality living! This is Hell!

Know God - Believe God - Choose God - Love God - Follow God!

An unplanned event occurred just as this book was about to be published. It had such a massive impact on Karen and me that I included it for your insight and hoped for discussion.

There are a few pages at the end of the book devoted to explaining what this was all about. It came about while sitting with the young vet at an animal refuge. Our 14-year-old cat Bella was diagnosed as too sick to enjoy life anymore. We three decided to take that horrible decision to end her life then. While we were waiting and chatting and holding a most beautiful looking relaxed Bella who was at peace, so close to death, we were given a unique experience of LOVE. I had never felt LOVE like this, out of what seems to be a negative option; yet in our heart of hearts, we truly believe it was the correct choice. Hopefully, our experience that afternoon may have some incredible loving impact upon others, especially you, the reader, as it did Karen and me.

Our 14-year-old cat Bella was diagnosed by the
vet to be too sick to enjoy life anymore.
We three, the vet, Karen and I, decided to take
that horrible decision to end her life then.
While we were waiting and chatting and
holding a most beautiful looking relaxed Bella
who seemed at peace,
so close to death,
we were given a unique experience of LOVE.
I had never felt LOVE like this, out of what
seems to be a negative option;
yet in our heart of hearts,
we truly believe it was the correct choice.
We told Bella we'd see her at home with God.

Author

Bryan has been married to Karen for forty-three years. They have three adult children and four grandchildren. Their two eldest children are teachers, while their third is studying for her honours in a science degree at university.

Bryan concentrates on his writings now, having retired from teaching in both the primary/elementary and secondary/high schools in August 2019, after 42 years of teaching years 1-12, including 30 years to year 11 and 12 Study of Religion students. Bryan's beliefs about God will be shared minimally in this Book 8A. He believes it is essential to any genuine love discussion to discuss all strong beliefs. Especially as we don't know what part God could play in our lives and the world in which we live at various stages of our time on Earth. If there is no God (as most secularists believe), nothing good or bad could be taken from this discussion by the secularists. Most religious people believe God is the centre of true Love and that we experience GOD through GOD's Love. Time will tell for each of us.

The main *Series* he is writing today began in 2016 and will conclude in 2022 with nine books and other media platforms. The writings include six nonfiction books, three photobooks, approximately 35+ YouTube videos, four websites, and three social networking sites. The websites and social networking sites will be worked on now but will increase output and details in 2022.

Bryan has played a significant role in schools. He taught for forty-two years and has been a primary/elementary school principal twice, once at Tara and another at Goondiwindi in southern Queensland, Australia. He was also an assistant principal in secondary/high school (for twelve years) on Queensland's Gold Coast. He has seen or experienced many lifestyles and beliefs coming from this city – the tourist capital of Australia, along with five trips overseas plus numerous within Australia.

Has the world become an insecure place for you these past few years? Are you feeling that your Love of various people and positive, loving lifestyles are becoming highly questionable or even threatened today? Is it becoming quite difficult in our developing or dying world with a massive population and an enormous number of personal and communal beliefs? And so many challenges need to be faced and solved. Does it appear to be infringing with violent or unethical responses from several countries and leadership groups worldwide on so many issues?

Do the various actions of different countries towards the Covid 19 pandemic seem to be telling you something wrong or even evil about some of these countries and other influential sources. There are still too many questions about Covid 19, its origin, and everything to do with the honesty of countries affected by the virus, especially at the pandemic's beginning. Who is lying or being truthful with their country's situation during Covid 19, including illness and death numbers and solutions for the world affected by the pandemic? There seem to be way too many queries about Covid and its place in today's world and the future's world. This scenario is very suspicious and challenging for many. Threats of severe illness and possible military or internet/digital attacks start becoming the norm. It is also now that Love takes a hit, and people often go within themselves and try and ignore or hide from the threats.

What is the absolute Truth of the questions surrounding this severe illness, a worldwide virus? Millions of people worldwide have been infected and are hospital-bound. Officially, over 5.5 million people worldwide have died from it so far. Covid has infected 290 million worldwide. Both statistics were correct at the time of writing. What is the actual, honestly shared number who have died and/or been very ill in ICU, etc.? So many questions! Was it an actual virus deliberately released into the worldwide community? Is it an act of war? Are various powerful military and medical state-run forces running real-world tests of the capability of the threat? Or could the tests be the attack occurring through Covid 19 now?

The world needs genuine, authentic LOVE right now! Urgently! Death and destruction are hardly the solutions. Greed and lies are not the answer.

Bryan believes that there is a significant need to bring Love back to societal leadership. (For many, this means getting God back. God is believed to be Absolute Love for most people and is needed so much by the whole world now!) Unfortunately, many in our society, believers, and non-believers, often make uninformed and questionable decisions, which have substantial impacts, many not favourable, on the world's populations. Sometimes, this may be due to misunderstanding the Creator's guidance, commandments, and teachings. Sometimes, a conscious or non-conscious devaluation of our generally accepted positive and supportive morals and ethics occurs. This may happen based on a person's limited appreciation or knowledge of various religions and the essential ethics and morality they share worldwide. Many believers also make similar decisions. These are often due to confusion, ignorance, lack of knowledge and facts, etc. Be accurately informed, whether you believe in God or not.

Depending on our personal beliefs, we need to question what we are to do as Loving partners, friends, and colleagues with or without our heavenly Creator? Obviously, these can change and often do throughout our lives. How can we gain from this? What does each person need to do?

All relationships are linked to LOVE in some way! Our Love becomes shared LOVE worldwide through our lived example and working together in the name of peace and Love.

This next book, Book 8, *Love is the Meaning of Life (2nd ed)* 2022, is the second edition of Book 6 and goes somewhat to the core of true Love and Love's place within our world. It is mainly done with an emphasis on secular, non-religious beliefs. For these people, what follows now in this discussion would be considered chiefly unreal and impossible! But is it?

The author believes that he received 21+1 Revelations from God on three different occasions, 1982, 2016, and 2018. These will be included in section 8B for those interested readers.

Book 4, a photobook primarily, *Where's God? Revelations Today Photobook Companion: GOD's Signs,* has incredible photos of special sun effects: sunrays, sun flares, sun arrows, a giant Easter sun cross in the sky (Book 4's cover image), a moonrise over the ocean, and double rainbows. No photographer has yet explained how these were formed. Bryan now believes that these were sent directly by God, mainly through the sun. There is an eyre of mystery and Godliness involved. Either way, these are spectacularly authentic images taken by the author. Often these weren't seen and didn't appear on the camera's image screen and were only seen when uploaded on his laptop.

There is a large amount of acknowledging that God is now in an era of Signs and Symbols. A recent Gospel and subsequent homily within a major Christian Church denomination discussed this in detail worldwide. This now confirms a significant point the author has been writing about since 2018. These sun, moon and cloud signs and symbols point to God's existence and the place and acceptance needed for oneness with God. These images are very spectacular and need to be seen to aid each person's decisions about God. Each print is totally genuine and authentic, with no 'photoshopping' changes or digital enhancements. Book 4, a photobook, contains most of these images. Titled – *Where's God Revelations Today: God's Images* (2018). Each photograph can also be seen on a few of Bryan's websites, including *bryanfosterauthor.com godtodayseries.com* and '*God Today*' Facebook page.

Believers may be very interested in something received by the author to be incredibly strong and influential, which affected him in 2016 and 2018. Books 1, 3, 5, 6, 7 and 8 explore the 21 Revelations received by Bryan from God in much greater depth. Each book covers various Revelations and Inspired Images and emphasises unique ones in more detail. However, going even further back in time, the first Revelation was received in 1982, when a school principal, a religious sister/nun, prayed over him on the school's 'Commitment to God' day. 'Tears from God' were received, as was the incredible warmth from his head to toes.

Books 1 and 5 have themes that should at least attract the reader's attention, whether you are a believer or not. And in some cases, these will vigorously challenge various religions and followers of those religions. The invitation is for you to try as much as possible to please be genuinely open to what you may hopefully find in these two books. You may never know if you don't give it a go! A deeper exploration of two key 2016 Revelations from God to Bryan is central to this *Series* – Revelation 10 – One God Only One God of All for Eternity – *1God.world: One God for All* (2016) (Book 1's theme) + Revelation 15 – *Jesus and *Mahomad are God* (2020) (Book 5's theme), i.e., both Jesus and Mahomad are Incarnate, i.e., God living fully as human prophets within our world, who return to Heaven as God fully (Book 5's theme). It highlights what Love is and how Love impacts every individual and community. (*Mahomad is spelled this way mainly in God's Revelations to the author.)

There is also a challenge for the reader to seriously consider the place of a higher force, or at least a possibility of this, in all loving relationships. Love is an essential phenomenon for the existence of humanity. It helps us be accurate, truthful, and loving. A much more complete humanity and Lovers of all things good. To also appreciate our need for others when difficulties arise. Many people believe that they can claim evidence of various relationships with the higher power we may know about. Love and its impact would come from a much higher force. For these people, our Love experiences are from beyond our ordinary world. Is it a higher force integrating with us? Is it a universal Absolute Love encouraging us to grow together as one people, one world - one totally with Love? (Those who believe in God - and are one with God, could see another dimension of the divine Love many want and need to experience.)

Love is the Meaning of Life – True LOVE.

Uppermost is Bryan's desire for us all to grow as close as humanly possible to each other and our world communities.

To assist as many people as we can in their quest for a world of LOVE.

(And for those believing in God, to reach the Absolute Love of God while still on Earth, and to become one with God's Salvation with people in Heaven, after the person's death.)

During these past 14 years, Bryan, and his wife Karen (Directors), produced and published their 25 books, including this *Series* of nine books, eight published with one to come in 2022, through their own publishing company, Great Developments Publishers, from the Gold Coast, Australia. Five school and church marketing books were also written or published between 2007 and 2011.

Bryan and Karen have a sideline interest as well. The author uses twelve photobooks, and many of the 780+ videos (YouTube channel – efozz1 and CaravanAus) by the author helps the beginning caravan owners care for and operate their caravan. They then explore great places to stay, see, and things to do throughout Australia. Each of which comes from first-hand experience. These have been very popular over the years. Each concentrate on locations throughout Australia for caravaners. Other campers and trailer owners are also finding these helpful. The collection comes from Bryan and Karen's various caravan trips throughout Australia.

As well as this sideline interest, there is a *Series* of 33 videos in Bryan's 780+ YouTube videos that cover this *Series'* theme. For believers, along with those interested in exploring these themes or are open to this approach, you will find that Bryan engages with the reader in the videos. This should help those interested in appreciating the All-Powerful, the Creator, who came to this world for us! If you care to read further, Section B will hopefully assist with the spirituality and religious beliefs and practices you may be interested in. This may be a challenge for some, but hopefully, one worth considering. The YouTube channel has two links - 'efozz1' and 'CaravanAus'.

Love 'Rules'!

Author's Academic Qualifications:

Master of Education (ACU, Sydney)
Bachelor of Education (ACU, Brisbane)
Graduate Diploma of Religious Education (ACU Brisbane)
Diploma of Religious Education (Institute of Faith, Brisbane)
Diploma of Teaching (McAuley College, Brisbane)

ACU = Australian Catholic University
McAuley College became the ACU
Institute of Faith = a faith educational arm of the Catholic Archdiocese of Brisbane

Author's Websites

For further information and reader response:

https://www.bryanfosterauthor.com/ (Author's website)

https://www.godtodayseries.com/ (Main website for this *Series*. Includes the blog commenced in 2016)

http://www.greatdevelopmentspublishers.com/ Publisher's new webpage. (Original website started in 2007, closed 12/2018. Now a new webpage)

https://www.facebook.com/groups/389602698051426/ (God Today - Facebook)

https://au.linkedin.com/in/bryanfoster (LinkedIn)

https://www.youtube.com/user/efozz1 - (780+ YouTube videos commenced in 2009 and covered various themes, e.g., God Today; Marketing Schools and churches; and many hints, tips, and places to stay for Caravan Beginners.)

https://twitter.com/1Godworld1 (Twitter being developed)

https://www.instagram.com/(Instagram)(1godworld being developed)

Book 8A and Section 8B

Introduction

8A - *Love is the Meaning of Life (2ⁿᵈ ed).* **Highlights the secular approach + key topics and points of consideration for appreciating Love.**

8B - *Love is the Meaning of Life: GOD's Love –* **Summaries of selected Book 6 key points to help balance the secular and religious/spiritual aspects of Love.**

Due to the nature of these two books, both discussing the statements that *Love is the Meaning of Life*, 8A concentrates on the secular appreciation of Love and Life. In contrast, 8B from Book 6, *Love is the Meaning of Life: GOD's Love,* focuses on the more detailed link with GOD being Absolute Love. Both 8A + 8B have been combined to clarify appreciation and understanding of many relevant discussion points in this latest book in the *Series*.

Section 8B summaries taken from *Love is the Meaning of Life: GOD's Love* includes key summaries from Book 6 in this *Series*. People who choose to read book 8A may or may not be interested in Section 8B. Section 8B is placed towards the end of this book. It is not Book 6 - but contains some important messages and beliefs from Book 6 for those wondering about or who want to know a good deal more about God and Love. Book 8A is the dominant themed book in Book 8, concentrating on Love and its quality. Book 8A takes a secular approach, and God is not the significant aspect of the discussion. Yet, several fundamental 'Love being God' points are included as a balance.

Bryan Foster

8A

What
is
Love?

Love is the
Meaning of Life

'What is Love?'

What is this Love we are all trying to gain and share with others? It is a way humanity can experience some of the unique, loving qualities craved by most people. For comparisons, I need to add that for believers in God, it is a force that puts all humans equally first with no favourites. It is up to us what we do with this freedom. The force is Absolute Love! Religious followers believe true human love to be that Love you are prepared to accept from the higher power, in most cases known as God, first and foremost before anyone or anything else. The other special people you Love deeply come next. When a loving couple believes that their partnership is indeed one, i.e., together equally in all that is Love, a permanent life commitment often follows, primarily through marriage or a permanent, secular couple relationship. There will be times when people believe in God or not. You become challenged to be open to the Divine. This book will be mostly about secular Love but will also jump into a place for God in these loving relationships; to assist you, the reader, with your questions, choices, and decisions. Just as for any significant life decision, it is best to be fully informed before any decision is made. There could, and possibly are, options you weren't initially aware.

This is not forcing you to do or believe anything you are uncomfortable with or about what you feel differently. Being fully informed as much as possible under the circumstances is one of the vital principles of and for this book and this *Series* as it should be for any highly contentious, challenging books or articles about these previously highlighted topics. Just guessing, or using your gut feeling, is only a small part of any decision made.

For believers in God and from the author's experiences of and with the Creator and All-Powerful of the universe, the divine power comes first in everything we do, think, feel, and Love! The higher force is a necessary part of any genuine appreciation of Love - being Love, as God is! God's Love, or a powerful Love we search for, is, or could be, the meaning of life for us! We are invited to respond to God's calling us to a measure of divine Love.

There are various levels of love in the world today. Because this word is thrown around so much, you would be forgiven for thinking that a 'perfect' strawberry or your family pet or career is love, e.g., 'I love my job!' Let's explore some of these explanations.

But firstly, let us consider - the 2nd world and 3rd world situations. Suffice to say, as may be seen most times on the televisions or other digital devices viewed by us on this topic or similar, is to see that the second and third worlds' poverty, lack of good services for hygiene, poor lifestyles and health, home inequality, insecurity, education, comfort, etc. have a significant influence on their lives. These are real dilemmas and difficulties for both the 2nd and 3rd worlds. Surprisingly for some, many of these people are relatively happy accepting their lot in Life. Especially when they feel a genuine closeness with God, this is no excuse to ignore or not help them in this somewhat cruel world of the poor. Most of us in the first world never or rarely have to experience or live this lifestyle and predicament! It is challenging for this world's people to claim they honestly and genuinely understand what the poor are going through. The 1st world must take a high level of responsibility for these people's impoverished existence. Social justice, genuine love for people (and God for the faithful), etc., demand that we must be significantly fairer across our globe. Hands up those happy to share their spoils! This includes those pleased to give up a level of most things until equality is reached. Until we can reply to these sorts of questions with, "Yes," there is minimal social justice and human rights and responsibilities across the world.

We, the 1st world countries, are generally failures at these times! Greed wins again. Truthfulness is also lost as it becomes hidden by the powerful and wealthy, along with others with various means. If we are hidden from the bad Truth – we can get lost and become one of them – claiming no worries from those who have so much - let's just get on with life as we are used to doing??? STOP!!! How can we do this to others? No one is entitled to any more than anyone else. That's the hidden Truth. We must acknowledge this and be proactive for equality.

(For the faithful believers in God, we can't even think that God won't know! Because God will understand. God already knows what you will do at any time in your Life. But you still need to do it, to make your own decision (whatever that is) when, where, why, how, and what. You still need to make your own choices with your own Free Will. This is how it works for God. God is looking out for as much love as possible from all people in all ways. Love grows within each person as you move towards God in your lives. Evil actions and beliefs move you away from God freely.)

(This next paragraph explores the place of God with Love for those believers and those wanting to experience what it is all about from a religious, spiritual viewpoint. For those who believe in some powerful force, a creator beyond our world, the highest order of Love starts with God/Creator/All-Powerful/etc. The absolutely loving Creator of the universe demands that our relationship with this entity is first and foremost and is the deepest of all loves. Most genuine religions have God as the centre of the universe; for example, we must love God in Christianity and all other genuine religions. According to their teachings, there is only one God in Islam, Christianity, Judaism, and Hinduism. It happens to be the only God for all religions and cultures forever. However, the challenge just begins because each religion believes in its own one God. A few believe that their God is the same as another one's God. Book 1 in this Series, *'1God.world: One God for All'* *(2016)* explores this concept in depth. In Book 1, people's experiences, including the author, scriptural quotes, and religious commentaries, are included for spiritual and personal assistance. This book also has twenty-six personal stories from the author to help us discover God in today's world through others and then through our individual life experiences.)

Those with a spouse or partner who is central to their existence would have the next level of love. This is the person they would 'do anything for out of love'. Of course, this is balanced with reality. The deeper the affection for this person, the deeper the commitment and, ideally, the deeper the reaction from the one loved. This may even be similar to the loving relationship with GOD for many people. This is often titled AGAPE LOVE - on a plane as close as possible for humanity to experience the Divine.

Children resulting from these spouses or partners are on very similar love levels as existing with the parents. The main difference is that the children are born from their parents. The love for these children is as good as the spouse/partner love without the most intimate physical relationships. Good parents would do almost anything for their children. Still, they should not spoil them, which would help them grow into gifted, well-balanced, and successful adults capable of impacting the world significantly in their lifetimes.

Family love follows. The extended family unit is usually the most passionate and supports love beyond personal spouse/partner/children. It is where the relationships are 'based' on blood. The DNA very much holds these groups together in ways not necessarily possible with ordinary friendships. Yet, things can go wrong because we are human and fail sometimes.

Friendships bear similar loving relationships but mainly on a slightly lower level. However, these may sometimes be unique relationships beyond ordinary friendship into incredibly good and healthy relationships. Friends forever could be a call! In general, though friendships are the next level. A place where each friend of yours helps make you the best person possible. You may sometimes feel that a friendship is as strong as a partner/spouse relationship. We must be careful not to allow anyone in any relationship to take advantage of us.

One of the most controversial loving relationships is with a pet and/or natural flora. Humanity seems divided as to how unique these relationships are. It is challenging not to see the love various pets display for their carer/owner and vice versa.

Pets such as dogs and cats (but not only these two groups) would fit this category in most instances. These animals' faces and parts of their bodies show various emotions. There does not seem to be any substantial scientific evidence of this at this level, only anecdotal evidence. Many of us would hazard a guess and feel exceptionally confident that there is love in our responses and those responses from animals and plants. Existing with flora often brings a more relaxed state to the people concerned. Most people would probably not acknowledge this, yet we probably have similar stories anecdotally once again. Plants and trees have a unique relationship with these people, whereby their natural flora domain brings a mere presence, which is genuinely rewarding for them. I usually feel incredibly close to pets, various other animals, and flora. Just sitting with most of these creations is exceptionally relaxing, as one experiences God's variety of creations given to us for our stewardship. We are responsible for the welfare of these living fauna and flora.

A memorable experience occurs at Crystal Castle in the hinterland behind Byron Bay, Australia. The video link below is of my wife and me reacting with various plants electronically. Music is developed through an attached synthesiser with two connection points on the plant being used – one goes in the ground; another is clipped onto a leaf. Many would dispute the truth/accuracy of this; however, you hopefully won't doubt what we did and what the plants did. The video shows these reactions well. There was a time when a plant I was standing next to had a leaf of it touched and held by me. The volume of the synthesiser went up considerably. Karen and I believe that the electronics (or something else) within the plant were being changed into music. Either way, it is a cause of discussion about the Truth; and what is real and what is fake. When viewing the video, you most likely will see the different reactions from the plants as their environment changes. For example, when the plant is sprayed with water, it seems to come more alive and react through the music; the synthesiser changes from quietness to an electronic sound.

The final level of love is for all those inanimate, lifeless objects and other emotions, which we all too easily name as love. For example, I love my pillow; I love my job. I love the holidays, etc. No one would dispute these being special, but these are not examples of love but more examples of 'like'. Love is a two-way response between living animals (including people) and plants. There is no two-way affair occurring in these other just mentioned inanimate examples. One way is not deep love, except when the primarily faithful believers agree that God's love for all of creation could never be matched on any level. God offers his LOVE to everyone equally. It is up to us to decide if we want, should want, and NEED God.

Another commonly used example of the 'love' term is sexual passion. When this is an integral aspect, one shares with their loving spouse/partner, it should take the relationship to a high level if treated genuinely, lovingly, and adequately. Loving passion is an integral aspect of any deep love between two adult people in a life-long commitment. However, this would be more 'lust' than love if it is purely a physical relationship devoid of the deep love just described. It is an example of how we are lustful with this other person. But it isn't the same as the emotion of love displayed in a truly loving relationship.

Let us particularly consider human Love and how Forgiveness and social justice are crucial to these loving relationships. There cannot be a genuinely loving relationship without some critical aspects of love being paramount – it starts with genuine Forgiveness. People need to be able to forgive others and themselves. These loving and forgiving responses to misbehaviours and other weaknesses, some being indiscretions and wrongdoings, all the way up to severe evil reactions or leading evil lifestyles, justify how we make authentic love truly real. Everyone needs to incorporate social justice / human rights within their loving relationships. They need to start with appreciating how all people are equal. Then to understand for the faithful, that in the eyes of God and/or each other, they need to treat all people with dignity, respect, and equality. The social justice and human rights enacted by all people at whatever level is required and capable of doing, allow true love to grow and flourish within themselves, their committed partners, families, and communities.

https://www.youtube.com/watch?v=7U_z0MUo4MQ

- ‘Music FROM the Plants at Crystal Castle (West of Byron Bay, Australia) – Unbelievable? But very probably True?

What is Love?

People have various genuine thoughts, beliefs, and experiences on this question.

What can we gain from others?

Secular people may see other kinds of Loving relationships occurring, with or without God's involvement.

_____

Those who want divine Love, need the depth ensured when adding God as # 1 to their mix.

The faithful appreciate how communicating regularly with God adds so much to all our Loving human relationships.

Having God always on our side in everything, especially Love i.e., the Meaning of Life, is a most incredible gift from God.

Believe it and experience GOD!!!

These secular beliefs are also authentic, but not believed to be as strong by the followers of God. As strong as would be gained from God's involvement.

'I Love You'

"You are the love of my life!" or "I love you!" etc.

How often have these remarkably enticing and impelling words been uttered throughout the millennia?

The utterers of such wisdom usually refer to their spouse/partner, parents, and children. On other levels of love are the different groups we 'love' – sibling, best friend or relative, etc. Yet, we can't include everything here. Otherwise, it diminishes the true 'love' we refer to and often tells the difference. For example, what level of love suits this list - Car? Smartphone? Cat? We can't love our dog anywhere near as much as we love our children. Children must be loved more than their pets. Imagine how out of skewer the world would become if pets were treated equally or better than our children, spouses, or partners.

This whole notion of life-long love with people is the basis for most, if not all, of our actions throughout our lifetime. Love is the ever-calling, ever-demanding positive aspect of our lives. Without love, who are we?

Love is not just philosophical discussion; it is the most inherent and integral aspect of our individual and communal lives! I dare say that we cease to exist as a complete human being without it. A person needs to interact not only with others but with the self. This person is on a real human journey. That is the point. We need to search through ourselves and our place within our community, to find where we fit into this most loving of places, in time and space, matter and energy, and most of all in spirit.

We must not lose sight of our spiritual side. Many influences from within the western world are trying so hard to destroy this aspect of our lives. It is trying to fill this with aspects of the 'big void', materialism and self-centeredness, etc. Yes, it is often complicated to admit to this occurrence. Yes, it is often challenging to even see at times. But yes, it is so vital for our soul, or whatever you want to call that aspect of life that ties us incredibly strongly to the one and only Creator (GOD) for all people, for all time!!! Once we accept these various forms of love and levels of love, we can genuinely grow in our love to be as close to GOD as possible. This divinely inspired growth should be our primary aim in life. One of the critical reasons for this is that the closer we are to GOD, the more robust and more realistic our love for others can be. As we experience a unique closeness with GOD, our priorities and values change to a higher level. We can love more vigorous and more efficiently than we could ever imagine. The place of others becomes a central aspect of our lives. An intimacy develops beyond the everyday belief in love to become a much higher order of love and one where GOD's creations, on all levels, are seen in a new light which glows.

Love is the ever-calling, ever-demanding, yet absolutely necessary aspect of our lives.

The closer we are to key people in our lives the stronger and more realistic can be our love for ourselves and others.

It is all about Loving and supporting those close to us.

Family Love

A loving family is the most vital unit within civilised and tribal groups. Family love is the most effective form of earthly love! It needs to be nurtured, supported, and encouraged. Successful families could be voluntarily evaluated and modelled on to help others without such depth of love. Otherwise, there needs to be a greater preparedness to share what works and what doesn't in mature loving relationships.

When each person truly loves the other, great things happen! Differences are accommodated, successes are celebrated, challenges are issued, respect is integral, and most importantly, Forgiveness is offered and received wholeheartedly, to name but a few actual outcomes.

A mother's love for her child. A husband's love for his wife. A daughter's love for her siblings. A son's love for his father. And the cycle goes on into an often complex and beautiful web of family relationships of love.

Family members are gifted with blood relationships. Nothing is more substantial or everlasting - except for creating a new bond between husband and wife, leading to the loving union creating children.

Out of respect for one another, individuals are encouraged to be themselves. To be the people they desire to be. These individuals will grow as people over time - even if the direction taken is contrary to accepted family norms. At times this will lead to challenges within the family, yet a genuinely loving family should have the ability to overcome most, if not all, challenges. Or at least get other friends, colleagues, or relationship specialists to help.

Family members will be open to challenges issued within the family: challenges to strengthen outside relationships; challenges to improve themselves in specific or general ways; challenges to be an integral and valued member of the family.

All within the family should celebrate successes. This will be difficult for various members to grapple with personal challenges, insecurities, and dilemmas.

When each member celebrates another person's success, they grow personally within and beyond the family. They grow in self-worth and love for the other. Once this is discovered, the whole family unit grows and is strengthened and unified.

Being forgiven is an awe-inspiring moment for any family member, especially if the Forgiveness is because of some extreme hurt from or against another within the family.

Society needs to model successful and loving families and not just accept without challenging dysfunctional ones. Dysfunctional families are real. Some would say the norm these days. A devoted friend, family member, or other society members needs to assist these families or encourage those struggling to improve so that each family becomes more loving within and beyond the family unit themselves.

Families are the strength of any society. The stronger the family is, the stronger the society. Society needs to encourage and support healthy, loving families and support those struggling.

Families are the necessary strength of any
society.

The stronger each family is in Love, the
stronger the society.

Society needs to encourage and support strong,
loving families,

as well as to support those who are struggling
and disadvantaged, who need our help…

We cannot ignore the calls from the poor!

To ignore these is to not LOVE!

We are always just one moment away from
death!

All of us must work, play, live and love
together within our community.

Love changes all

Once someone knows and appreciates true love, their whole approach to life, self, and others changes. Love changes all!

It is often frustrating to see people's emphasis on being superior to others or continually trying to be better than others, all for their perceived self-gain. It is time these people stopped thinking that because they had good fortunes and opportunities in life, they are somehow owed something special and what others have received on life's journey who were not as fortunate.

They may have studied for many years. They may have spent all those extra-long hours at work: day after day, week after week, year after year - investing in the future. They may have sacrificed all those family hours for their career and a considerable income. But in all reality - so what!?

I, too, did once happily justify all those extra hours at university, at work, and away from family. I, too, eventually saw reality and the realisation that the golden earthly rewards were mostly an illusion compared to what God offers freely, out of genuine Love.

What counts are the relationships of love. Love for self, family, and all others within our world.

I realise that certain people will see these claims as a 'pie in the sky' philosophy. It certainly did for me - once.

How often do you hear from those who have stared death

down in the face or those who complete a total life change that all the money in the world, the most incredible job in the world, the most fantastic lifestyle in the world all mean nothing relatively compared to those loving relationships that count in that person's life - i.e., the most incredible family and friends in the world!?

Unfortunately, consciously or subconsciously, many people see 'friendships' as a business proposition. You cannot buy a loving family and friends. If it appears that you can 'buy' friends, then, unfortunately, these are not real friends for the right reason - these are the people who usually expect to gain something from the friendship. These people see it as an investment, which will reap the rewards for them in the future.

Once you reach the happy, loving disposition, it becomes easier to add the subsequent layers of relationships to the mix - the community you live in and the world in which you are an integral member.

Once I had a car, which I thought was the most remarkable feat of engineering possible (as you do?!) - and it seemed close to that level for me? After driving it for a few weeks and getting over that initial love affair with an inanimate object, I began to wish that all people could drive such a car. I did not want to be the only one with such an opportunity. I wanted to share the experience. I did not want to be so special and feel good about myself because of something I had and others did not have. Sharing life's opportunities and rewards with others, enjoying their joy and yours, is so very special for all concerned.

Being aware of the 'istics' is part of the journey. This was when I realized that I had matured from that youth-filled person years ago. That love is about sharing with others. I did not need to be so materialistic and individualist, and all those many other 'istics', which I had initially thought were the answer! Life is much simpler with the necessary needs. We confuse the complexity instead of the simplicity required with enjoyment and life fulfilments.

This is the start of an incredibly freeing experience:
• the desire to share with others
• not being someone, due to someone else not being that something
• everyone's right to have love in its most fundamental sense in their circumstance - in its loving reality.

Love changes all! People need to appreciate what love truly is - people and relationships take priority. The previously mentioned 'istics' have no significance in a genuinely loving world! A few do, though, e.g., holistic and wholistic. That is, holistic people, radiate that holy love that comes from GOD! This profound GODly love now experienced can significantly change us if desired.

Once someone knows and appreciates what true love is, their whole approach to life, self and others changes.

Love changes all!

Love is Celebrating the Success of Others

True love enables people to celebrate the successes of others.

When people experience what love truly is, they love celebrating others' successes - not for themselves but for those who have achieved success. In this situation, the person who has achieved feels a sense of accomplishment, while the other feels happiness and joy.

It's no longer just about me – but about everyone!

Loving people will encourage and support others to achieve success in their lives. They will be there on their journeys, subtly offering necessary advice, etc., but always out of utmost respect for the other person. At no stage will they make the person feel inferior but will help them feel equal. Through this respect and subtle guidance, a genuinely loving relationship should grow, and out of this, the other will feel worthy and successful.

Why is it that so many people have difficulty doing this? Is it jealousy? Is it a lack of personal self-worth? Or maybe it is a competitive streak that sees no bounds? Perhaps it is even that people don't realise that it is crucial for successful relationships. They may not even know that it is fundamental and necessary?

For whatever way it is, these people are missing something extraordinary, often because of negative life experiences.

These people may need assistance to build their self-esteem, self-worth or appreciate where competitiveness begins and ends. The growth process invariably takes considerable time. After all, those who experience true love have, more than likely, developed to this stage over a substantial amount of time - often over many years.

A loving person will consider all this and accept where those people may be at any time in their lives' journeys. A loving person will not judge these people but will support and encourage them through the challenges they face.

Being able to celebrate others' successes is a true sign of love! Being able to do so naturally - without question and without looking for something in return - is a high point of love!

True love enables people to celebrate the successes of others…

In this situation, not only does the person who has achieved feel a sense of accomplishment and valued, but the others feel happiness and joy also.

True support. True LOVE.

Lifelong Friends are Forever (LFF)

The value of lifelong friends, particularly those formed in the early years of life, is beyond this world. Don't many of those special friendships that began so long ago mean so much now? Overall, the years and experiences of some friendships defy the test of time. GOD has given us some exceptional people for some extraordinary reasons. Often, initially, we aren't even aware of these reasons!

Often due to these experiences' intimate nature and the life-changing ones shared over such an extended period, these special friendships may even be on a similar level as a family. Because of this, people need to appreciate the uniqueness and specialness these allow to be shared.

Some people trap others to treat these extra special friends with too much familiarity or disrespect. Being very close to someone often affects people to hurt the other person knowingly or unknowingly easily. Familiarity breeds contempt, sometimes.

How often is it that the ones we love we hurt the most?

Having special friends who last a lifetime is something beyond the everyday. These are friends who would often do anything for that friendship. Never abuse this possibility. Never take advantage of these few, extra special, loving relationships.

Treasure these special friendships like diamonds – rare, beautiful, unique, and worth every dollar. There also may be times needed away from each other for some energising and refreshing of the relationship. This is good and helpful. Use it wisely.

Love is Giving

Love is giving to others. When people love people, they provide assistance, advice, time, finance, etc. When a person is genuinely in love, giving to their partner/husband/wife/children/ parents is a natural aspect of their partnership.

When people are very much in love, they get to a stage where they want to give more than to receive. Or close to this level of giving. That is how many people get to know that the one they want to share is that exceptional person - the person they would like to commit themselves to for their lifetime.

We then have love being shared in everyday life. People help family members, community members and groups, the sick and dying, the disadvantaged, and the suffering from inadequate provisions for a healthy life. Political prisoners, corrupt unions, companies, and governments, cause much angst and often result in unjust effects on the average citizen.

If most people on this planet decided to love their fellow humans, then equality would become more possible and actual for many millions more. Our Earth has enough materials and resources to supply every person with enough to live a reasonable quality of life if we so choose to share. This shared wealth would lead to a more peaceful and loving world, as those without them gain greater equality and have fewer problems to attend to daily. It then becomes a time to love and share with humanity. Greed needs attending to for this outcome to eventuate.

Love is Giving – Especially When Times are Tough, and Catastrophes Occur

Love is giving of ourselves and other vital aspects of our lives. This is mainly shown through a lifestyle and the quality of friendship and community welfare displayed by the populations. Most countries have suffered these catastrophes requiring a large population's assistance. The level of success varies considerably worldwide – often dependent on community attitudes, skills, and finances.

I want to highlight a couple of significant challenges in Australia over the past few years, of which I am well aware. And these are examples most countries also face. These challenges are worldwide, with different countries often reacting differently to similar tragedies. Yet, each country tries to save as much property and life, human and animal, and flora, as possible. One example, for simplicity, is in the coming together to help those in need and seriously affected. Australians know this as mateship, as demonstrated throughout the flood-covered Queensland eight years ago, or the massive fires Australia-wide in 2020. Australia is a country of extremes of climate. Any year, it is usual to have many extremes, e.g., droughts, floods, cyclones (hurricanes), and bush fires. Many are often covering thousands of square kilometres. Examples are the raging bushfires of 2019 and the many droughts from 2016 to 2019, etc. Dates vary for individual places across the continent.

2020/1 saw the pandemic COVID-19 severely affect many countries. Over five million worldwide died, and tens of millions were infected. (Accurate at time of writing, Oct. 2021.)

In Australia, for something considerably different, all states Health Ministers and the federal government's Prime Minister and Health Minister (and other key people as needed) combined to form a new and unique national parliamentary ministry to plan and implement the pandemic's various stages. The federal parliamentary committee made multiple decisions, with each state government's health departments and premiers department. There were specific border closures decided by some states, while others may not have come to the same conclusion. The actual quality of decision making varied considerably, unfortunately. Most decisions were of good quality overall, though. Unfortunately, some other countries weren't as well led or prepared for such incidents, and neither could many of these be in the light of their daily struggles and lack of money and investments. Many countries need specific help financially, and first world counties are helping these emerging countries out significantly. Towards the end of 2021, five optional vaccines are available worldwide. Most governments are administering these well by now.

These occur quite often, sometimes yearly. Since the above significant floods, fires, droughts, other floods, cyclones, and naturally destructive events have also occurred.

Catastrophes occur such as motor accidents, violent attacks, diseases, and pandemics, through to such things as power outages as supplies are cut, plane or other crashes, etc.

These are just a few examples of giving unconditionally to others during bad times anywhere worldwide. Volunteers are usually a significant number of helpers. We all have stories of other nature and catastrophes, causing severe problems and causing many sacrifices from those affected directly and indirectly.

Many examples exist worldwide, so I'll explain the significant flood already introduced as a relevant example to help place these 'Generous volunteers' in perspective - the first responders are the obvious go-to's when these events occur. They may be paid or be volunteers.

One absolute hero was the dad of a student I taught in year 10, who, as firefighter and rescue personnel, was one of the first volunteers to be sent to the Christchurch, New Zealand's destructive earthquake. His job was to crawl through the wreckage, often collapsed large city buildings, find those trapped and arrange for their rescue with the rest of his team. That was exceptional true LOVE for his fellow humans.

The major flood eight years ago, literally covered three-quarters of my state, Queensland, Australia, over three weeks. As a comparison, floodwaters in Queensland have covered: five times the size of Great Britain, or twice the size of Texas, or four times the area of Japan. The state capital city, Brisbane, was severely affected during that time. The Central Business District (CBD) was shut down when power was cut for days.

Thousands of volunteers, including older school children, helped throughout Queensland, assisting those whose houses, businesses, schools etc., had been damaged. Neighbours were freely giving time and goods to others who had been flooded. People are travelling between cities and towns to assist. The coordination of search and rescue, rebuilding infrastructure, keeping up morale and volunteers, etc., led by the state's

Premier and country's Prime Minister, has been outstanding. Even though Australia is a country of excessive natural disasters, such as floods, bush fires and droughts, etc., no one predicted anything like this. This is by far the greatest natural disaster to hit the country and our world for a very long time. Yet, it virtually paled insignificantly compared to Covid 19 and especially the Delta variant.

About a half of Australian mining resources are mined in Queensland, and a similar percentage of various agricultural goods are grown in this state. It usually takes months, if not a couple of years or so, for people to rebuild their houses and businesses, for the public infrastructure to be repaired or reconstructed, and for the economy to return to normal.

However, the true Australian spirit of mateship, of giving everyone a go - no matter their nationality, religion, career, wealth, etc. is prevailing - and prevailing very strongly! That's LOVE.

TRUE LOVE means giving! True love is not about taking! In times of absolute turmoil and destruction, true love is seen as honest and visible. These floods have brought out the best in people. Thousands and thousands of volunteers are currently doing just this. The good news is that very little looting or crime has occurred during this period!

The thousands of people who have been directly affected by this catastrophe have likewise been helping others in need. Flooded neighbours have helped neighbours, towns have helped towns, and cities have helped cities. That's LOVE.

The recovery bill was well into the 10s of billions of dollars. Special thanks go to all the people throughout the country and world who have been generously giving financially to assist - this is love in action. Money is critical to the successful rebuilding program - for people's lives and public and private infrastructure.

Australia is one of many countries famous for its generous spirit of mateship and genuine camaraderie. People genuinely value others, especially in their times of need during hardship and struggle. It is such a pleasure to witness this in action - TRUE LOVE wins!!!

Most people react similarly worldwide to various natural and 'man-made' disasters faced by humanity. When a person has empathy for others, helping others in their times of need is considered essential and the norm. They TRULY LOVE their 'neighbours'. Often these people react to a questioning person or group of the unsympathetic with disbelief. They would answer with something like, how could you not help those in need? How could you be so selfish? If they were named as heroic for their assistance, the typical reply would be along the lines of, I am no hero, anyone would do this to help their neighbours, etc. They would add, real heroes are those firefighters, air-sea rescuers, police, ambulance, and paramedics, to name but a few.

When a person has empathy for others,

helping others in their times of need

is considered essential and the norm.

They TRULY LOVE their 'neighbours'.

TRUE LOVE

True love means giving!

True love is not about taking!

It is particularly in times of absolute turmoil
and destruction that true love is seen as

real and visible.

Often, Love 'saves the day' for many.

Love and Forgiveness – Essential for Love

Love and Forgiveness are both essential for True Love!!! Most people find Forgiveness the most challenging aspect of love. To forgive others and to be forgiven ourselves is quite a challenging experience! Yet, this is essential for the repairing of any loving relationship.

Once we can forgive others and forgive ourselves, we are on the way to living in that reality of love again - the meaning of life.

Not being able to forgive, or be forgiven, tears away at our very selves. We may feel less of a fully human person. We feel damaged and sometimes even irreparably so. We feel that love is less in our lives or even missing.

Some people will claim that Forgiveness is not always necessary. That time will heal all wounds. That all we need to do is to get on with our lives. I believe that on most occasions, this is just a cop-out, a search for an easy way out - yet not a real solution. (Unfortunately, some circumstances may lead to this through unexpected realities, e.g., loss, departure, or death of one party involved.) Even if most of the hurt can be forgotten with time, there is always some remnant of damage, inescapable pain, somewhere in the conscious or subconscious. This pain will invariably surface in the future, most likely when a similar circumstance prevails, as was originally the hurtful situation.

We need to offer Forgiveness if we are the perpetrator of the harm. We need to take that most challenging step to begin the process of recovery and reconciliation. When we offer Forgiveness, the person who has been hurt has the opportunity to start the process of returning to love.

Suppose we are harmed, and an offer of Forgiveness is not forthcoming from the other person or group of people. In that case, we may need to expedite the situation by diplomatically giving them the chance to begin the reconciliation process. Diplomacy is often the best method; however, a more direct approach is necessary for some people, but still needs to be done out of love, in a caring and respectful way.

When we are offered Forgiveness, we have the opportunity to begin to or be reconciled. We need to accept the offer as soon as possible and repair the relationship.

The process may be quick and clean. However, it also may take time depending on our personal history with the person involved and their personality.

We often need to forgive ourselves. This can be quite difficult. We need to learn to accept our own Forgiveness and move on, just as we do when accepting Forgiveness from others or when we offer others Forgiveness.

Forgiveness is a crucial aspect of any loving relationship. To forgive allows the relationship to return to its proper loving place. Forgiveness is Divine.

Love is Social Justice for All

'Let's be fair about this!' 'Give a mate a fair go!' 'Don't 'kick' the down and out!' 'If not for the Grace of GOD, there go I…'

How often have you heard these sorts of comments? How often have you thought about helping a friend or someone unknown to you? How often have you yearned to help someone less fortunate than yourself, just out of your Loving humanity? I guess we are challenged by these comments or thoughts quite regularly. These thoughts are good, but the crucial point is what we do about the ideas!

How much love must it take to help an unknown, especially if friends or family challenge your actions? Why do good people have an inherent desire to help others? Is it because it is universally the right thing to do? Is it because it is Godly?

I believe it takes a special love – a true love - to do this: to help someone you do not know, to help someone when your friends encourage you not to help, and to help someone who truly needs your genuine, authentic, and very truthful assistance!

It saddens me greatly when I hear over many decades' selfish comments, such as:

'Every person for themselves!'

'It's a dog-eat-dog world out there!',

'The only person who counts is you!'

'Don't help them. They are only using you!'

'If you don't look after yourself, no one will.'

'If they were serious, they would help themselves/get a job/have a bath/etc. be seen as respectable everyday people.'

Real love desires to help all people immensely. To significantly help your family. To help your friends. To help others who need our help. To help those who do not have what we have! All this is relative! How can we help, or do help, depends so much on our circumstances? That's love!

Watching television and internet shows, which display how people who have so much yet also have an inherent need to help others, react, etc., is quite compelling, along with those who have very little and, regardless, still do help others accordingly.

I often wonder if these individuals are more concerned with being noticed publicly through the media 'for their good works of charity' or whether they are doing the television show for altruistic reasons, and are very interested in motivating other people, particularly the rich, also to become active participants and givers for those in need. I tend to think that both sorts, and more, become involved in such shows. I also know some very wealthy people who do not want any limelight associated with such shows but wish to anonymously give the considerable needy amounts of money and time.

We all need to commit to genuine acts of love beyond our own safe, everyday environment. Yes, looking after family and friends is usually of primary importance, i.e., very important – so is helping those in desperate disadvantage. We only need to look to those ideal models we see throughout history to see that looking after our private world is not enough! Consider Jesus, Gandhi, Mother Theresa, and others, such as Bill and Melinda Gates and other extremely wealthy people in many ways, with or without money, as classic examples of people looking well beyond their comfort zone.

Consider those people you know of, or have heard about, in your area where you live, who do so much for others. Consider how you would feel if you joined these people to assist those in need within your neighbourhood, town, and city.

My favourite charity is 'Rosies: Friends on the Streets'. This group of exceptional volunteers, like many other organisations worldwide, assist those in need on the streets in major centres, in this case, throughout the east coast of Australia.

The silent voice is an unheard cry from the needy, the poor, the ill, the lonely. These assisted people who have so little means are not heard beyond their immediate existence by the noisy self-absorbed to helping those in need close to where they live. We need to show true love initially. Let us all 'come' together to assist as many needy people as is possible – always remembering to keep a balanced healthy life. The sick or injured can't help the needy properly if suffering themselves.

The voice of the silent is an unheard cry from the needy, the poor, the ill, the aged the weak and the lonely...

These people who have so little means are not heard beyond their immediate existence by the noisy, self-absorbed, selfish world.

To show true love, let us all commit to helping those in need in any way we possibly can...

Let's start with those suffering and close to our own home – our families and friends.

Consider those people you know of,

or have heard about, in your area where you live, who do so much for others.

Consider how you would feel if you joined these people to assist those in need within your neighbourhood, town, and city.

.

Why do descent human beings have an inherent desire to help others?

Is it because it is universally the right thing to do?

Could it be God's love or something else carrying us forward?

What about those who don't desire to help?

Is it their problem???

Is there a part we and others can play, in both the problem and the solution?

The Meaning of Life is LOVE.

"We are One."

We are all equal – an example

This incredibly challenging article has been included to invite as many interested readers as possible (with respect) to go beyond the relatively publicly unchallenged secular beliefs and be challenged to consider some extraordinary and mostly unique God experiences, as I experienced personally in 1982, 2016 and 2018. Anyone can experience God if God so desires. Prayer is essential to gain God's closeness.

I have included this article because of the most empowering, authentic experiences I have ever had in my life. In 2016 and 2018, I legitimately had God send me 21 Revelations while I was camping on the plains of Mt Warning/Wollumbin in northern rivers NSW, Australia, early in the morning around 3 am on both occasions. God asked me to write these down both times and to be very accurate. To then get these distributed as worldwide as possible. This led to my *'GOD Today' Series* of nine books, 2016-2022. Book 9 is the final and is out in 2022.

I realise this chapter's title's belief/statement is not accepted by many people. But because it is the believed Truth from God by the faithful, the ramifications are enormous! It is Revelation #8 from God to the author on 29 May 2016 – "We Are One". Book 1 followed this incredible spiritual experience and began the distribution of these Revelations as advised by God – *1God.world: One God for All*, 2016, written by Bryan Foster.

(Book 3 should also be referred to for standard links with the topic. *Where's God? Revelations Today*, 2018, by Bryan Foster)

As I sit here waiting for my BBQ to cook at the showgrounds in Canungra, just outside the Gold Coast where I live – so much becomes very apparent – once again. This is a widespread realisation now!

Ever wonder why so many say – "Oh, I could never go camping/caravanning/RVing… I'm a 5-star person…?" Because it is in these outdoor environments where so much becomes apparent, these camping caravans, motorhomes, 5th wheelers, etc., bring most people present closer together.

I sit here tonight [a few years ago] after my dad's football team Richmond had just won the men's AFL grand final, their first in decades and something he will never know due to his dementia. Observing those around me, camped next to me are two ladies, one whose husband went to the game in Melbourne today, over 1000kms south, along with her mother. The younger lady has a beautiful Mercedes parked outside her mum's caravan. Across the way are two ladies and a dog, both with older cars. Over the past couple of days, both arrived independently of each other. One had a male who assisted; the other came on her own. Both are in small, quite old caravans.

Yet, there is an authentic realisation that we are all equal amongst these apparent differences.

There is a beautifully balanced noise of discussion and enjoyment of life happening all around me. There are many more than described above. Many families with children on this last weekend camping before the school term resumes this week.

Let us all stop the pretence that we are better than anyone else.

Stop the pretence that because I have worked so hard, and maybe have taken so many risks and succeeded, that I deserve all my gains, and others don't. That I am successful, and they aren't! Wrong!

Most others have also worked extremely hard, taken risks, etc., but not 'fallen as well on their feet' as the privileged few have landed. This doesn't make them any less 'successful'. If people were honest, they would have to accept that there is so much 'luck/fortune' in people's successes. Or they have been born into wealth and/or privilege, nothing to do with their skills, etc. It is so much easier to start life with money than with no money! Who would disagree?

Stop pretending that any of us are better than others!

Oh yes, this does invoke numerous rather challenging outcomes. Yes, we may need to re-evaluate where we stand on this equality issue. It will challenge us to become better human beings! Yes, we will have to give more to others. No, not just your family or good friends or professional colleagues, partners, etc.

Unfortunately, this is often far too great of a challenge for those with much. They believe they have 'earned' and 'taken so many risks' for it all that they don't need to assist!

WE ARE ALL EQUAL – Once we can accept this egalitarian principle, then –

THAT'S TRUE LOVE!

We must stop believing that we are better than others or others are better than us!

Share!

Genuinely believe in each other equally!

Assist! Love!!! Enjoy!

True LOVE is for All!

You'll be a special person with others who Love authentically

+ with GOD also for believers!

Stop the pretence

that because I have worked so hard,

and maybe have taken so many risks and succeeded,

that I deserve all my gains, and others don't.

That I am successful, and they aren't!

Wrong!

Humans feel the same inherently – until…!

The billionaire president of a first world country, the poor in third world countries, the sick person in a hospital, the dying, the beautiful model on a Vogue cover, the Olympic champion, our neighbour, our parent, our spouse/partner, all feel the same inherently as each other.

Human = Human.

All desire the best possible. All feel as human as each other. Everyone on this Earth feels the same intrinsically!

We all want LOVE. Happiness. Necessities. Good education. Good health. Successful occupations and careers. Successful lifestyles. Security. Freedom. Justice. Forgiveness. Etc.

It doesn't matter what we look like, our wealth, our career paths, our family, our religion, our culture, etc., we all have the same inherent human appreciation of who we are as a person.

That is until so many unforgiving forces tell us differently – i.e., along 'comes' the 'real' world! By the way, this 'real world' is not necessarily how people claim it to be.

Various things change for everyone. We suddenly get affected by so many destructive views that we may lose our genuine appreciation of who we are. We may no longer appreciate much about our true selves and others.

The media and various social platforms echo or create so much societal negativity. The 'screaming' consumeristic devotees, along with the inherent doubt and vulnerability of the human entity, are often the worst instigators changing our self-perception and how we feel about ourselves on any given day.

The internet trolls who aim to harm others are evil at heart. This is not something people are born with; it develops in individuals, most likely resulting from considerable negative experiences in their lives. These days more than ever, possible mental health issues may develop.

Over time and with wisdom and experience, and heaps of decent people, friends, and family, we hope to discover our true selves once again. Our LOVING, generous true selves must come forward!

_____

Many people, if not most, believe that God, or some other eternal, powerful, divine force, wants us to feel and be truly loving, healthy, beautiful, appreciated successful individuals, no matter our varying cultures, religions, and circumstances.

According to the Revelations from the God/All-Powerful/Eternal, I firmly believe I received 21 Revelations overall in 2016 and 2018 while camping on the plains of Mt Warning, NSW, Australia. It became my Sacred Site. If anything of outstanding quality came from these Revelations, it is this Revelation #8 (and #15 explored later) from God to the author on 29 May, 2016 – "We Are One"! Meaning we are all one and equal to each other. We must never forget that we are equal in God's eyes and that God is always there to assist every one of us. All we must do is ask! Ask, as we should do very regularly, as we all NEED God so much! Why? Because we are not divine but human creations from the blessed, perfect, and Loving God.

(*Where's God? Revelations Today*, 2018, by Bryan Foster)

Be prepared for the unexpected when communicating with God. Be open to various solutions and support from God, with some options not being expected by you. Trust in God and God's ways. Listen in your heart of hearts for that exceptional communication with God. That special message or feeling. That solution is to help you through the tough times when God will be carrying you.

Be prepared for the unexpected when praying with God...

Trust in God and God's ways.

Listen in your soul of soul for that exceptional moment of communication with GOD -

That special message or feeling.

That solution to help you through the tough times when GOD will be carrying you.

There seems to be a strongly held belief by most people worldwide that GOD is Absolute LOVE.

Be open to a Loving GOD. Ask for assistance from GOD. Love GOD in return.
If genuine, your life will change in many ways for the better. That is GOD's way!!!

The Gifted, Talented, and Fortunate OWE the World out of Love

To be fully human, our gifts, talents and fortune must be shared within and without our societies. Sharing raises the levels of happiness for all. The greater the gift, talent, wealth, beauty, etc., the more significant the sharing demanded of all those people! The responsibility to assist others must be very high for them.

We are all equal in God's eyes (Revelations #9), and hence the need to LOVINGLY assist and raise the quality of others' lives to being equal in the world's eyes is called for by God. Social justice is the cornerstone for this equality.

To be free, each person needs to be an active, positive, sharing, respected member of society.

Those who choose to hide away and bury their gifts, talents, and fortunes will never be truly content or happy. They will often fear losing and concentrate on retaining or increasing this. This egotistical and selfish approach often leads to despair.

The good in all people is crying out to be freed. For selfish, negative reasons, people don't release the good. The fear of having nothing or having less, of losing the gifts, talents, and fortune, is an extraordinarily robust and negative motivator for the ego and vulnerability fact within the human entity.

Everyone's role is to improve the quality of those suffering, poor and disadvantaged. Whatever gifts, talents, and riches we have, we need to share these with others in a constructive, community-building way. We must use our God-given talents/gifts/riches, etc., to improve the world and those who live within it. Greed and selfishness are the main destroyers.

Caritas explains the eight social justice principles.

See website: Our Principles | Caritas Australia

Caritas is a worldwide organisation that aims to help the poor, vulnerable, weak, powerless, etc., to work towards equality with all other people of our world.

We are all equal in God's eyes

(Revelations #9)

hence the need to LOVINGLY assist and raise

the quality of others' lives

to that of being equal in the eyes of all, which is called for by God.

Social Justice is the cornerstone for this equality.

(See the 8 social justice principles above)

Have a [GOOD] Heart – Our Personal One

My whole appreciation of life changed, having watched the ABC (Australia) 'Catalyst' episode, 'Heartbeat: The Miracle Inside You'. A show with awe-inspiring messages, vision, and straightforward explanations. (The YouTube internet link for the show is at the end of this article.)

An Australian heart surgeon, Dr Nikki Stamp, is brilliant as she takes us on a genuinely lifesaving journey. This is so relevant for all those with hearts! (Bit of humour there, I hope. I get this way when overtaken by brilliant medical science – especially info., which helps save valuable lives!) Those with heart issues or the capacity for or physical flaws have heart issues. (No matter your age and lifestyle, you may not even know you have problems!?)

Indirectly, it also shows the awesomeness of the creation of the human heart! Some of the statistics will blow you away.

For those open to the real miracle of life, you cannot help but see the place of the Divine in all this.

As iconic Australian presenter Molly Meldrum used to say on the musical TV show 'Countdown' – "Do yourself a favour! - And watch it if you haven't!"

Watch ABC Catalyst show – 'Heartbeat: The Miracle Inside You'. Dr Nikki Stamp explores the world of our hearts. She explores their operation, what we need to do to take care of our hearts, and explains the latest science used in surgery to repair damaged hearts. (ABC)

(Catalyst: ABC iview for Dr Nikki Stamp's heart explanations.)

LOVE in Nature (e.g., Oceanic Dolphins and Surfers)

LOVE can be experienced through the natural world's experience of LOVE. GOD/LOVE is the absolute creator of life and can be especially experienced in our natural environment.

Swimming, or observing up closely wild dolphins and whales, brings out something quite remarkable in us. The 'Tears from God' experienced simultaneously through these encounters marked these experiences as incredibly memorable and life-changing for me. I have been very fortunate to have had two close and personal experiences with dolphins. One was a dolphin purposing just a couple of meters in front of my surf ski ride as I surfed across a wave. Another was two dolphins swimming upside down and around my seven-year-old daughter and me just off the beach in waist-deep water. This is part of the dolphins fishing routine, so they become more invisible to the surrounding fish swarming above them. And ended with one upright circle, the normal way up. This was to the point of experiencing something beyond our earthly existence. Tears flowed, along with the 'OMG', 'Oh My God' feeling in its most authentic, spiritual, and genuine sense, as these dolphins circled us one sunny, summer morning at Kingscliff, NSW, Australia.

LOVE is there in nature, hopefully within our typical day to day lives, for all people to experience and with which to engage.

We must be open to it yet need to be in an actual loving state to engage fully with it properly. There are so many ways to experience LOVE.

The twelve most common ways to experience genuine LOVE, I believe and have discerned, are through:

- Spouse, children, and family
- relationships and work colleagues
- best mates
- our spirituality - personal and communal
- nature lifeforms
- pure and positive leisure, activity and physical time
- creating things – leisure, work, domestic, neighbourly
- sharing deeply and forgivingly when needed
- giving to others, not just receiving
- life's freely chosen vocations – something liked personally and fulfilling. Work hard to achieve it.
- music and song
- God - Initially to ultimately

However, due to everyday reality, God is so superior to us all - totally. LOVE develops all levels of LOVE experienced by us as people. God creates opportunities for all forms of LOVE. Just ask the Creator for help to be LOVING. Be prepared to give and take what is genuinely and LOVINGLY offered to you.

An incredibly personal experience of surfing with the dolphins in the wild of the ocean was one of the most majestic experiences of love in nature that I have experienced. It occurred at Broken Head, near Byron Bay, in northern New South Wales, Australia.

My first experience of dolphins, up close and personal and away from the local dolphin tourist attraction, was surfing on my short surf ski at Broken Head, near Byron Bay, Australia. Byron Bay is an eclectic beachside township, primarily a holiday and wealthy beach lifestyle destination, especially for backpackers worldwide. It has a strong, diverse spiritual undercurrent and welcomes people from the extremely rich to the old-style backpacker/hippy. It is also a world-renowned backpackers' haven - quite a fitting place to experience what turned out to be a most spiritual occurrence.

This was to the point of experiencing something beyond. Tears from God poured out while riding the crest of a wave on my short surf ski a couple of decades ago. This creation of nature, a dolphin, and I extraordinarily met that day. The cosmos seemed so small. We were ONE at that moment in time! It appeared to LOVINGLY lead me along the rather large wave, porpoising a couple of metres in front of me. I did everything to remain in this moment, even though both tears and fast spraying water made seeing quite tricky. God was in, and with this dolphin and me.

On that day, I was surfing amongst some extremely beautifully formed turquoise waves, with many schools of dolphins porpoised through, over and under the waves. On one giant wave, I was speeding across its front wall of water and had water spraying into my face at such a speed that I had to keep blinking my eyes to avoid the spray obscuring my vision. I had just come out of the tube/barrel of a wave when a shadowy black figure slid through the face of this wave's wall of water to my right and went downwards underwater in front of me. At this stage, my greatest fear was that it was a shark and all the horrible thoughts of such a situation flew through my imagination! Panic set to such an extent that I feared to fall off the ski - but knew I had to fight to stay on, no matter what!

At that moment, the shadowy figure quickly rose to the surface immediately in front of me, at about two metres, and porpoised up and down - virtually leading the way! I followed, mesmerised by what was occurring in front of me - I now dreaded to fall off out of absolute awe of this most enjoyable dolphin experience! And miss all the exhilaration which was forthcoming.

Tears and water filled my eyes - and blurred my vision but not the sheer enjoyment shared with me! I was indeed in the most LOVING zone! I was one with nature - with a most remarkable, intelligent mammal, this wild but gentle dolphin – both of us seemed to be enjoying each other at that one moment in time on a shared wave. I subconsciously fought to maintain my balance as I was distracted and in quite a euphoric state. This dolphin, a most remarkable creation of nature with high intelligence, and me, exceptionally met that day. The cosmos seemed so small. We were ONE at that moment in time!

The literal, physical sign of divine LOVE given to us by God, 'Tears from God', permeated these two most beautiful, awe-inspiring experiences. LOVE in nature is real. It is also part of the meaning of life. LOVE is experienced within and outside the natural world in many all-encompassing and enfolding ways.

Many of us have stories like these which have left a remarkable memory and experience of nature and God. Mine was in the ocean, but others will also be the ocean or anywhere else that the soul exists, maybe as well.

Throughout our lives and our world, LOVE is there for us all. We must be open to receiving and giving it. Yet, we need to allow ourselves to be LOVING to experience it properly. We close ourselves off from it when we desire not to harm instead of to others and ourselves. We also have LOVE closed off when others psychologically or physically hurt us. Damage to self and others may be in so many ways.

Live a LOVING life and LOVE will truly be

there within you and

with those you impact upon or mix with socially.

I was one with nature - with a most remarkable,

intelligent mammal -

this wild but gentle, safe dolphin.

Both of us enjoying each other

at that one moment in time in our shared wave…

On another occasion two dolphins circled my youngest daughter and me three times while waist high in the surf.

This was SO SPIRITUAL!!!

FORGIVENESS Highlights

Forgiveness of others and ourselves is Essential and often Needed.

Live a **LOVING** Life.

(With God? Or another All-Powerful Entity? Or Not?)!!!

LOVE is so real.

LOVE is the purpose of life.

LOVE is the Meaning of Life.

LOVE and **FORGIVENESS** are essential together.

Bushland Spirituality Aids Love

Nothing beats the bushland (nature) for spiritual balance and personal equilibrium. We all should have at least one place where we can feel at home spiritually - be this in the natural environment or some human-made (holy) facility for us.

It is through this that we can improve our loving relationships. Quiet, reflective time is necessary for a balanced approach to love and life.

We are very fortunate to have a few places which fulfil this need. Mine are primarily in Australia and Canada. The two places where my children live.

Australia's craggy features, uneven but robust gums, upright and rigid Australian grass trees – whether lush or burnt, golden red sunsets, eagles, dolphins, etc. etc. etc. and especially the resilience of everything standing and beneath – inspire and refresh!

My 'birthplace' of North Stradbroke Island (Straddie) is these and so much more! Is your birthplace special for you? If not, what is your place?

These past few years, I have been extremely fortunate to have spent a week or two each year on Straddie (Island), North Stradbroke Island, in Moreton Bay off Brisbane. Spending time there is refreshing, developing and personally becoming one with the Earth and nature.

Driving along the long white sandy beaches and sand tracks in a 4x4 RV, watching the brilliant nighttime sunsets, walking the trails and gorges, watching the whales, dolphins, and other exotic marine life on high and at close range, relaxes the mind and 'soul'.

Staying close to nature on camping grounds adds another new depth to these experiences. These days, camping grounds cover people's options at various stages of their lives, from tent camping to large motorhomes, fifth wheelers, buses, and eco-cabins.

Canada's magnificent Canadian Rocky Mountains regions' rivers and creeks certainly bring nature to all those who access it. Like other countries with significant mountain ranges and snow-capped mountain peaks.

These are genuinely natural and beautiful experiences in all that is our oneness with the spectacular natural environment!

For believers, the Divine is present in these regions and geographic features. The natural magnificence from streams to the mountains is repeatedly loaded with 'Wow' moments. It seems that every corner on every road into the Rockies holds another 'WOW' moment. All this comes about through the lifeforce each human, animal and plant possess. We sense inherently this very close association with other Divinely created lifeforms. We enjoy their presence with us. Even the wild attacking types attract us from in a caged enclosure.

Nothing beats the bushland for spiritual balance and personal equilibrium.

We all should have at least one bushland/watercourse place where we can go and feel 'at home' spiritually…

All this comes about through the lifeforce each human, animal and plant possess.

Love's Challenges

Introduction to Love's Challenges

Something so good as True Love will often attract incredibly positive comments. Otherwise, some very cryptic negative ones could come from others who hurt through the lack of genuine love in their lives. A genuinely loving person will ignore the minor negatives and concentrate on the positive. Yes, there could be much hurt and pain in either reaction, especially the negative ones. However, a loving person will see the deficits and the 'hurt' and 'pain' in the negative people. Empathy often leads to heartfelt sorrow and a need for healing by those who feel the pain and are so affected.

Empathy is Love!!!

As society grows and matures, it takes on each relationship's specific positive and negative characteristics, from a loving couple to a community and society itself. As this century progresses, so do the types of relationships and individuals develop. Couples may now be of the same gender. Same-sex marriages are now legal in several countries worldwide. Transgender people and their partners are also present in our society. All people need to be respected and included, however possible. We are all equal. (Revelation #9) With this freedom, though, comes specific responsibilities. No one can harm another for any reason unless in self-defence.

If possible, and primarily due to the actual reaction to the negatives, giving them your forgiveness and allowing and even encouraging them to turn away from their hurtful and demeaning comments, responses, and their lifeways is what true Love inspires us to do.

Some of the most difficult challenges for those searching for or trying to keep Love in their relationship/s begins with the full awareness that all people are equal. Many do not accept a belief, including the selfish, ignorant, indulgent, entitled people. Depending on their reactions and attacks, these could be genuinely and seriously evil. When people think or play the 'I am better than you' card, you know difficulties will arise, maybe even immediately. These are not loving people in these circumstances.

Social Justice Principles and Human Rights are two evident leadership principles, which highlight what is socially acceptable, along with evil/destructive behaviours. Along with all other levels on the continuum.

Combine these with varying levels of influence from the media, perfectionists not allowing for all levels of Love, ignorant people, the secular world often believing in their false power and influence, bullies wanting their way, etc.

If possible, and mostly due to the actual reaction to the negatives, giving them your forgiveness,

and encouraging them to turn away from their hurtful and demeaning comments, reactions, and their life ways,

is what true Love is encouraging us to do for others

(and ourselves, at times).

Human Frailties Affect Loving Relationships

To love and be loved is the primary purpose of our whole existence. Love is the meaning of life. Why do so many people allow all the other lifestyle issues, values, resources, relationships, etc., to get in the way? Why do so many people let the distractions interfere and often dominate their lives?

Most people would believe that the desire to love and be loved to be an intrinsic part of life - you are born with it. You are born to love and be loved. People who live a balanced life love others within their family and friendship circle. I sincerely appreciate this message. Once this message is appreciated and lived, it becomes the standard, accepted practice to relate to others and everything Loving about our whole world.

However, many get distracted for so many reasons and then lose that proper focus somewhere along the way. The human frailties of greed, selfishness, envy, failure to forgive and be forgiven, lust, gluttony, etc., come to the fore and seductively entice people to follow this distracting and destructive pathway.

This transfer of priorities may even occur in early to mid-childhood, where parents or other significant adults or people within the young person's life, live an alternate destructive lifestyle, e.g. illegal drug consumption, which is seen by the young person as the norm, and hence worthy of following (even if subconsciously). This unhealthy lifestyle then becomes the acceptable standard for living as they grow up.

People may then follow this pathway until challenged to do otherwise. Challenged to see the destructiveness of these chosen ways, challenged to confront the situation they then find wrong, challenged to become a better, more loving person. This challenge often comes at a time of complete lowness/loneliness within their lives.

To love and to be loved is essential for a successful life. It is the primary and quite raw need of all people. It is not only a fundamental emotional and social need of each person, but it is also the main spiritual desire and need.

Appreciating that Love is the meaning of life brings with it the challenge to love and to be loved in all its manifestations. To not get distracted and damaged by allowing all the other negative stuff to get in the way. This belief should always be at the core of all institutional religious philosophies, leadership, and theologies.

When *Love is the Meaning of Life*, the future holds no bounds. Love rules! Most people would believe that the desire to love and be loved is an intrinsic part of humanity.

When 'Love is the Meaning of Life',

then the future holds no positive bounds.

Love rules!

Perfection – being physically perfect!?

Why do people try so much to be perfect? Especially in the physical appearance stakes. There is nothing wrong with people aiming for the best possible, yet we need to realise that this is never perfect. To accept whatever happens to be the best at that moment or period is necessary.

The problem arises when aiming for perfection. Many become way too passionate about the expected result. To become so excessive in the attempts being made that the aimed-for results harm the person. In this Instagram/Facebook/YouTube/Spotify/Twitter/TikToc etc., digital world, the young and the elders are using so many apps/software at their disposal to 'create' who they want to be and pretend that this is who they are. 'Photoshopping' becomes so needed that the person is often unrecognisable or strangely different in the finished image.

Then we have all the body surgery available to change our appearance if we choose this; again, often to be unrecognisable. Some of the work done on people makes them often look fake or a strangely reprofiled human. Many seem to thrive with this unnatural appearance, often because their social group does likewise. Each person within their group supports the others, often unreasonably, given their changed appearance.

There is so much that has changed for these people physically and emotionally that their self-esteem and self-worth either take a hammering after the surgeries' evaluation of the finished product or the look screams out that this person is having real problems. For them, it is not who they are 'inside' but who they portray on the outside. It is self-worth that helps with self-esteem. That is what needs to be essential for everyone.

It is disturbing to hear adolescent-aged students justifying their make-up being worn at school, and often used excessively, as essential for their self-esteem and hence must be allowed to be worn. This claim is sometimes extended to school staff responsible for behaviour management of their students, supposedly causing mental health issues to the adolescent if they were stopped from wearing the make-up at school. Is this a school issue starting point for the whole person's appearance, which leads, in time, to the surgical process? Be careful, parents – it is your responsibility, not the school's. Don't blame the schools!

I wonder how much of this is related to parents who automatically get their children's teeth straightened or adjusted in various ways by specialist dentists. Perfect teeth are not a necessity. Unless, of course, their teeth or gums have significant problems and need adjustments, which is fortunate for those who have the financial means but still does not necessarily lead to 'perfect' teeth.

Virtually everyone knows that the pressure on various demographics is the backstory to so much of this problem. New and old media are once again at the forefront. It appears that many do not legitimately care about the damage they are causing – it's all about sales of products on their media and word of mouth in the real world. It often is not the well-being of the people to whom they sell for these surgical options.

As time goes by, more and more people who have had enhancement or 'personal improvement' surgery etc., discover that all is not good or right. Various medical issues may develop over time. Infections may have begun, movement or leaks from internal parts may now occur, the ill-fitting internal prosthesis is changing and developing awkwardly etc. Psychological responses may also be growing. These may help create poor self-esteem leading to horrible outcomes, including suicide.

No one can be perfect.

It is beyond the skills' level of Humanity.

Perfection is for the Divine only.

Aiming to be the Best is Best!

It is Real because we can often be Better.

Yet, Aiming for Physical Perfection

Can be dangerous.

Operations and lifestyle choices can go wrong.

Mental Health Issues Develop,

Poor Self-esteem can easily Build into personal Hate and

possible injury or even Suicide.

No
ABUSE.
No-One
Ever
Wins

Abuse = Hate = EVIL

EVIL = Anti-People/Anti-Creation/ Anti-Love…

LOVE = those who Truly LOVE

There is **NEVER** any reason at all for abusing anybody, for anything, anytime!!!

ABUSE = FEAR, PAIN, and SUFFERING FOR THE VICTIM

… & often for the **PERPETRATOR** ('if they have any humanity' and Love)

LOVE! LOVE! LOVE!

MUST WIN!!!

Abuse is Never Right

Abuse is for losers and bullies! The unwanted of the world.

There I said it. I realise this is probably not a good politically correct statement – but it is the case. It is true!!! Sometimes we must stand up for the Truth no matter how PC it may or may not appear. These days it is beyond the 'sometimes' and is now into the 'probably' in certain situations.

Anyone who must abuse someone else has lost the plot. They are acting and deciding with evil. More than likely, they have low self-esteem or at least a low level of options to solve the problems they believe exist in their lives. Or they may be highly intoxicated or drugged. Or they may be one of those who has suffered this sort of abuse themselves when either a child or in another relationship, which now significantly influences their behaviour as an adult.

The abusers often need considerable assistance due to the circumstance/s in which they became abusers themselves.

While society seems to brush over the possibility or probability that abusers could have been abused themselves, we will never be able to meet this violent challenge head-on. Why is this crucial point ignored or played down?

We all need to know how our experiences have impacted us and will probably affect our responses when we are older. An abused child will sometimes see this behaviour they were forced to endure as the actual norm for them and others like them when they are older, consciously, or subconsciously. This must be faced as a reality so that the abusive situation can be solved.

"Fear rules – often from the cyberworld – eliminate this…"

(Revelation #12 to the Author in 2016)

(Detailed in the 2018 - *Where's God? Revelations Today*, p.107-109)

While society seems to brush over the possibility or probability that

abusers could (or would) have been abused themselves, at any age,

we will never be able to meet this violent challenge head-on.

Stop hiding from the reality of where it often starts!!!

Be real.

Bryan Foster

World Security needs the young, specially to read/hear/see the news and know what is happening worldwide!

Over these past few years, it has become evident that most young people, and many of their parents, have very little understanding or appreciation of world or national events. This includes in their own country, town, and 'backyard'. Many sources exist which support this statement. My secondary school experiences as a teacher/leader totally agree with this premise. It is upon these experiences that this section is based. Also, as we progress through time, it becomes more apparent that fewer adults rely on credible sources for their news. Instead, their social media platforms supposedly meet their news needs – as do their children likewise! Beware! This could be dangerous and lead to many negatives for the unaware people and their societies.

When a young man in Melbourne, Australia, can falsely justify that his stabbing attack on two police officers was religious, it was based on ignorance. This eighteen-year-old claimed that the Australian police were attacking Islam. Any informed person within this country realises that this is not the case, far from it. Now is the time to wake the young and, in many cases, the older from their slumber.

And here lies the problem. Where is the Love? Be informed to make the correct decisions based on the facts. That is LOVE.

Most information the young acquire is resultant on their social media contacts and readings/viewings. Very few read the newspapers or credible news-on-line sites. They are basing their 'news' on often like-minded people to themselves, without much appreciation of the reality. Due to the nature of social media, this ignorance is then echoed and multiplied across their forums, timelines, videos, chats, etc.

As a teacher of high school students, it became apparent that this is a significant fact that the adolescents themselves acknowledge. Their response is often nervous laughter, a sign that they realise that their ignorance of news is an unfortunate case.

On delving further, it is often found that they have little time to check out the news. Their lives are filled with electronic social media, games, study, school, p/t jobs, and the like that regularly observing the world news is impossible. There are only so many hours in each day.

Parents and other adults also seem to be moving away from a full appreciation of the news. This incorrect modelling impacts significantly on the young as well. Ignorance is breeding ignorance. Be fully informed about our world? Yes, please.

It is very disappointing to see so many espouse the view that news is negative and that they, therefore, have no time for it. We need to instil in these people the notion that we need to be fully informed about critical worldly events, which may or will impact us. Therefore, we elect our political representatives and need to know what is happening and who would best represent us in civic leadership.

The young and others, who have continuously moved away from the informed and checked news cycle, need to be challenged to return to it. Proper decisions can be made for the security and peace of all when we are all informed about those issues affecting us or our world.

Ignorance is breeding ignorance.

Lifestyle Becomes a Distraction from Love

Let's start with the obvious – how we live our lives has a massive impact on how our Love works with others and ourselves. Authentic, genuine, honest, and serious Love is what people mostly expect and for which they aim to give and receive from others.

How we receive it from others, and ourselves is the burning question. Are we capable of developing loving relations all around us? Or are we too greedy and selfish to share anything of significance or benefit with others, especially sharing our highly valued Love!

How we live our own personal and communal lifestyles, in general, are at our whim. (Yet, there will be specific outside influences that impact us at varying levels on how we should behave and live.) We must make the correct lifestyle choices for all whom we love and who influence us and whom we influence. As well as for those especially on the fringes of our lives or are general career or student colleagues, etc.

At this stage in the considerations, we also note that if we want good, wholesome, and loving relationships, we must be cautious and open to distractions in our lifestyle, which could severely impact our Loving lives. These distract us from the all-important positive, loving lifestyle we need and desire to lead.

These distractions could come from a multitude of forces and influences and affect decision making significantly. The choices may be complex or confusing. There will be options.

Bryan Foster

Social Networking Sites May Cause the i-Generation to Become Superficial

Digital Revolution Side-Effects

The digital revolution has had a disappointing side-effect. Many young people, the i-generation (internet generation), have developed a superficial appreciation of world events, news, and other essential formation details, through multiple social networking sites such as Instagram, YouTube, Facebook, Twitter, Snapchat, Tic Tok, etc. The broadening of mind and spirit is highly challenged by the euphoria of the internet and all the engagement that happens while silently and privately seated before the computer screen!

No longer do many of the young keep abreast of the latest happenings in the world. The main priority for many of the i-generation is downtime. Leisure time is to catch up mostly on past, present, and future social experiences through their internet chat rooms and social networking sites, particularly with their friends.

The news, current affairs, documentaries, and family and friends' time take a back seat, if not being rejected as of any importance whatsoever. Significant time is spent on the internet, with the occasional viewing of television for little more than movies or sport. Everything is available on the internet. Adolescents can show you virtually everything, e.g., what sites are big, etc.

If the news is not broken through internet conversations within the limited sphere of influence of engagement of each young person, then rarely would the news and other mind-expanding information occur.

Twitter Revolution Challenged

The Twitter revolution of limited information, compacted into brief snapshots of what is happening to and for an individual at a particular moment in time in that person's life, becomes almost cathartic. Even when that person reports an item of interest to the world, it requires the young to follow that Twitter or receive the tweet through others who may be interested, and secondly be interested in such 'news'.

Through my experience with educating the adolescent, I would propose that the i-generation would, in most cases, ignore such events and get back to the social news of importance to them individually - their friends and associates' 'news'. Or the spectacular video options on YouTube, etc.

Social Networking Sites May Cause the i-Generation to Become Superficial - The Answer!

Television stations and other media outlets need to engage the young through the young people's, i.e., effective forms of communication - social networking websites. They need to promote their mind-enhancing stories to encourage the young to look further into what matters in this world. However, time must be given for those i-generation networking activities. To take this away would be detrimental to success.

Parents need to awaken the hearts and minds of their children to go well beyond the internet's social networking sites and engage with the real life-enhancing news, documentaries, and quality family time. Many parents need to set the tone through example, which in many cases is not happening now.

The i-generation, the first generation to live totally in the i/e-world, needs leadership and example from families, schools, government, and society. If they keep growing in their current direction, many of our young people will be trapped in a world of simplicity and unreality. They end up not appreciating the true wonders of life and the world, not knowing what really counts and is of importance to them presently as they mature.

Their operating model is so limited that only the truly gifted, talented, and broadminded amongst them will operate in society successfully.

Conclusion

The present situation sees the young i-generation challenged implicitly to awaken to the real world and place their special euphoric interest in social media sites into perspective. The place of Instagram, Facebook, Twitter, YouTube, Tic Tok and other social networking sites needs to be exemplified by responsible parents and families, teachers, and society. The young i-generation mostly appreciates the reality of both the digital and real worlds.

'Hate Speech'

Impact on an 18-year-old from Canberra, the Australian capital, and an Islamic refugee.

Amazing how one person's enlightened statements are someone else's hate speech!

Haven't we descended quickly? Not long ago, you were able to have enlightened discussions and free thought and publications about almost anything. Then came the politically correct ways of engaging and speaking, and a certain amount of freedom went away lawfully. Now we have polarised views on some very critical areas of civilisation.

Generally, no longer can we speak freely without being seen as hate-filled by someone else. This isn't just or loving – social justice demands righteousness for all, along with different opinions, beliefs, and practices. Gone is respect for a variety of views. Gone is respect for the individual. Going or gone are some of our God-given freedoms.

The prevailing notion also confronts us that because we can have our own opinion, that opinion is apparently correct – no matter the facts! If it is not factual, it is not valid!

Two stories stand out and bookend this view. We have a Somali/American author, Ayaan Hirsi Ali, having her honorary degree offer revoked in 2013 due to supposed 'hate speech'. Then a few years later, we have a young Canberra lady dismissed for being a 'No-voter', which caused her to be labelled as a person of 'hate speech'. All she did was legally vote against the views of many. Very strange for such a free and open country - freely available to all opinions, if not evil, genuinely hateful, or violent, etc.

Madeline, the 18-year-old lady who voted 'No', was an espoused Christian lady from Canberra who was sacked/let go/released from her contract (depending on reports) by her employer for supporting the 'No case' in the same-sex marriage debate. Why? Because this automatically defined her as stating 'hate speech'.

Voting no is homophobic, according to various same-sex marriage advocates. Highlighting your opinion is also supposed to be hate speech.

In 2015 Ayaan Hirsi Ali, author of '*Heretic: Why Islam Needs a Reformation Now*', a Somali refugee and Dutch parliamentarian, was offered an honorary degree by Brandeis University, Waltham/Boston, Massachusetts, USA. This was until six months later when it was revoked. Why? Following an online petition organised by the Council on American Islamic Relations (CAIR) on change.org. The accusations of 'hate speech' were enough for the revocation. Admittedly Ayaan's views may be excessive and highly challenging to many in the Muslim world, but these come directly from her actual oppressive experiences. She is no longer a Muslim but now is a fellow at Harvard University's John F. Kennedy School of Government.

Democracy depends on free speech and vibrant, robust debate. There is little cause for siting 'hate speech'. Yes, it does exist and needs to be called out when legitimate. Most claims of 'hate speech' are no more than someone with a different viewpoint being labelled to discredit his/her opinion.

Once we could argue and disagree, now it seems too many are way too quick to claim 'hate speech'! That practice is hate-filled in itself! Everyone must be free to add their own genuine thoughts and opinions in respectful and loving ways, no matter how different to the majority or significant others.

In general, if the [young] keep growing in their current direction, our adolescents will be somewhat trapped in a world of simplicity, unreality, and digital games.

Not growing to appreciate the true wonders of life and the world. Or what they need to be aware of, or challenged by, to be safe and secure.

They will not fully know what really counts and is of importance to them presently and as they mature.

Are these young, ambitious people of the democratic world, able to be prepared for disaster? For war? For protecting their countries when needed?

Madeline, an 18-year-old from Canberra,
http://www.theaustralian.com.au/.../9fb76f1b9f080a729aed
ccb42...
http://www.abc.net.au/.../same-sex-marriage-survey-
ca.../8958176

Gender Challenges

Male, Female and Others' Psyche. + Coherent Family Structures, etc.

One of the most fundamental differences we need to include in our chosen lifestyles, friendships, marriages. etc. is the differences and similarities of the genders. The most apparent differences are the physical differences. Being sexual beings, these gender differences are the most potent forces and should lead to great loving relationships in families and communities. Respectful physical, sexual, and emotional power can lead to much happier lifestyles and relationships.

Each gender should be authentically prepared to assist the other genders to appreciate their maleness, femaleness, and humanness in their growing relationships with each other. Each needs to understand all sorts of gender differences. This is where a problem begins with specific individuals. Those not comfortably aware of their sex and sexuality may find it challenging to listen, discuss and believe these. Yet, communication is necessary for any loving success. As a family begins with husband and wife and grows into a family with boys and girls as children, interactions between each family member take on their own appearance. Families need to develop roles to assist with a unified and loving family group in real action. These roles will undoubtedly change over the children's time at home and into the future when they eventually leave 'the nest'. Coherent family structures are essential for a successful, loving, and unified family.

Male, Female, Others and Family – Some Challenges

Males, females, and others are often challenged to take particular roles within their families and society. Often these are based on historical roles according to the various cultures and practices over history. These then get challenged in today's world with more politically correct and non-discriminatory options. Because families operate much within the walls of their housing options, many people don't know how specific ones work and what could be gained from the various options family-wide. Significant discussions are needed to find the right fit for each family.

We must be cautious about how we approach these roles and their place within each family because families have numerous impacts placed upon them. Usually, the parents consider the options and decide on their positions depending on their family, relationships and impacting others' experiences. These, at times, will conflict with those living around them or from their workplaces or various institutes, etc. But private commitments and roles for each are essential. Otherwise, chaos may result.

Significant discussions need to occur before co-habitation commitments begin. Similar conversations would emerge as required throughout the shared environment over their lifespans.

Physiologically and emotionally, the genders have similar but sometimes different thoughts and beliefs on approaching relationships and lifestyles. But one size does not fit all.

The critical starting point is Respect. Nobody should enter any form of lifestyle decisions, especially within families, unless this is done truthfully. Communication claims need to be open throughout such relationships. A couple of noticeable and slight differences would be that males often emphasise and feel well-placed with the security and financial dependence of their families. Except now, they need to allow for their partner/wife also to work and feel empowered with the family finances and security. Otherwise, the ladies usually have genuine motherhood needs and caring thoughts and choices to make in life. Also, it often has to do with financial and security options, especially for those that work. Parents need to be prepared to 'take turns' with parenting their young children at home, while the other works for the family's income if this is their choice.

As children grow within each family, they need to be educated throughout their lives initially through their responsible parents. All decisions need to be fair, with no one missing out or sometimes caught up in family politics. Children must be respected by all family members, just as it should be for their parents.

A family which shares mostly everything within their microcosm of family life should be more successful with the Love being shared throughout. A genuine family where each member is loved equally by the others and is treated so should be a strong family most of the time.

Remember that mistakes will occur, often not being deliberate, and these shouldn't be held against the perpetrator out of spite. Forgiveness and positive communications are essential for any relationship, especially the family.

Use personal mistakes to help make the family stronger.
Forgiveness is essential.

Love is crucial and needs to be seen as it truly is for each family member.
No one is perfect.
No one is privileged.

If each person treats the others as equals, needing similar things as the others, and sharing these likewise.
Over time, the family should be well on the way to being very successful and supportive of all members.

Indigenous First People's Challenges

HOPE Urgently Needed for Many of Our First Peoples Worldwide

HOPE Urgently Needed for Our First Peoples. (As an example, in Australia, the Aborigines make up 3.3% of the population.) Most countries have problems trying to solve their first people's issues.

Hope is the basis of all people's love and successful lives.

Hope to love and be loved fully. We hope to have beneficial relationships throughout our lives. Hope to be respected and valued. Hope to be forgiven and to forgive, including of oneself.

Many hopefully hope to find God in a hectic and distracted world. Hope to enjoy God's creations. Hope to reach salvation with God. Etc.

Often, they feel squashed, disrespected, unworthy, and hopeless. Let us explore the situation for the Australian indigenous peoples. On average, one Australian Aborigine a week has committed suicide over the recent years; many were children and adolescents.

Anyone travelling to or through so many of our country's towns will often see the hopelessness in our first people's eyes and demeanour. Karen and I experienced this in 2014 when we travelled up the Stuart Highway from Adelaide to Darwin via Uluru and then across to Kununurra in Western Australia. I would imagine from all the reports and feedback being offered to us these days that the circumstances are still horribly the same.

We felt hopeless while observing these people's hopelessness.

The answer from someone so grateful for having had so much in this life is that we as Australians have never really understood why the hopelessness amongst our Aboriginal brothers and sisters is so intense.

Some basic personal thoughts follow. However, to make these relevant for the aborigines in these townships, we must have aboriginal locals as part of the whole planning, managing, employing, and other necessities needed, especially with its implementation for their people.

From an outsider's perspective, let's now ask the locals of each community and township what needs to be done for there to be:

1. full employment, i.e., meaningful jobs for all
2. better education, i.e., as high as possible for each person from preschool to university or TAFE
3. improved health and social welfare services
4. agreed to housing, allowing for the first people's preferences and needs
5. safety and security for all
6. fuller and longer lives. Etc.

We must be cautious not to limit the possibilities for each person. We must encourage these people to support and help each person achieve whatever is personally possible for vital well-being, as high as for other everyday Australians. There are <400 Aboriginal doctors today, Australia-wide. (Source: 'The Drum', ABC television, 2019.)

Nothing is impossible for all first people to have similar opportunities for enjoyable, high quality, successful careers and lifestyles – which they choose!

A quite common situation is to find a country's first peoples often living in despair. This lack of hope frequently results from little or no employment. Or employment that does not suit these people's choices. This problem leads to many other associated issues, usually lacking self-esteem and personal/collective worth. This is then manifested through unfortunate behaviours and life choices, such as alcohol and drugs, health, housing, education, abuse, etc.

As is the case for many cultures worldwide, the general population of this egalitarian nation, Australia, very much supports the equality and uniqueness of our first people. They very much desire these people to have all the expected opportunities of every other Australian. Successive federal and state governments for decades have poured billions of dollars into various schemes to assist these first peoples to become more equal to the other non-indigenous people. Unfortunately, these schemes most often, deliberately or not, ignored the wishes of the indigenous people or were not fully informed as to the needs of these peoples and were more paternal than realistic. Often the financial management lacked skills and processes. These indigenous must be allowed, in fact, strongly encouraged to become a significant part of any assistance process, ownership and management... Usually, it could be claimed that the infamous White Australia policy was once again being implemented here, whether explicitly or implicitly, throughout the ages.

What was observed in the towns along the main route from Adelaide, South Australia, to Darwin in the Northern

Territory, and west to Kununurra in Western Australia, were financially poor indigenous people with minimal employment opportunities? People who were wandering around, looking for something to do. Most of these towns are isolated from the larger towns and cities of this huge, vast, dry land. It is common knowledge within Australia that the Australian aborigines lack opportunities for equality with the rest of the nation in the critical areas of health, education, employment, and even the law, as seen through the way out of proportion incarceration rate. Significant questions about laws, incarceration, mental health, personal and communal pride, living primarily in disadvantaged communities, etc.

Key aboriginal elders and those other non-indigenous Australians who either live with or provide employment must be listened to seriously in any policy formulation and implementation. Former policies need to be evaluated with proper and essential key aboriginal input. No longer can Australia flail about searching for successful strategies, policies, and laws.

The apparent observation within the towns visited on this trip was poverty and a lack of employment opportunities. Towns did not have the employment opportunities or transparent infrastructure to support the number of indigenous people and others in these places. Without a proper job and income, so many other difficulties arise. Poverty was rampant. Housing was poor. Poor health resulting from poverty and a lack of hope, both physical and mental, may have required assistance but was not overtly evident from the outside. Education success is challenged often because of poor attendance or the lack of hope in any future opportunities leading to limited years of schooling or any level of tertiary study.

Employment options seemed limited for aborigines, especially in towns and areas with shared aboriginal ownership or leadership, such as Uluru (Ayers Rock). The great majority of people employed in the township resort and businesses adjacent to the actual iconic Uluru rock, along with the cultural centre precinct at the true Uluru rock, were non-aboriginal! This seems quite extraordinary. I do believe this now ebbs and flows, between Aboriginals and other Australians, though.

There was also a view expressed that many aborigine locals living near mines were employed in those mines and after some time decided to leave their positions, live off their earnings and basically remain unemployed and mainly socialising within their local communities, often within their nearest town. However, this was not a common situation on the journey undertaken. Most places visited on the Stuart Highway, and others did not have the option of mine work. Yet, this would be genuinely valued where it existed.

There is currently a movement in its infancy within Australia challenging lawmakers and the general population to think and act beyond the square and failed historical policies.

Australia must offer its indigenous aborigines, our first peoples, a truly shared role in deciding how to support their needs. To carefully listen to the elders of these communities to formulate strong, valid, and intelligent policies, which will bring about an end to the lack of hope which appears to be found in most aboriginal communities.

Employment opportunities for Australia's first people will lead to a feeling of self-worth, the need to have their children educated, to look after everyone's health better, with the assistance of local health services, and to keep out of trouble and prison because family and community life is seen as so necessary to community members. The elders need love and genuine respect, and higher levels of control. The young need love and genuine assistance and guidance from their elders. Love both ways is critical!!!

Employment opportunities for the world's first peoples will lead to a feeling of self-worth,

the need to have their children educated,

to look after everyone's health better,

with the assistance of local health services,

and to keep out of trouble and prison because family and community life are seen as necessary to community members.

The elders need respect and higher levels of control.

The young need love and genuine assistance and guidance from their elders.

Love both ways is critical!!!

Love Solutions

Introduction to Love's Solutions

Love is so much more than lust, dreaming, desire, sex, etc. Love is something compelling, life-supporting, and life-changing. It is primarily an emotional characteristic, with solid physical and spiritual aspects – a meeting of the minds, hearts, and bodies. Don't let it just fall to sexual relationships. Love is far more intense, fulfilling, rewarding and beyond such simple needs and basic desires.

When everything is purring along with each person doing what is required to support their loving relationships, including continually trying to improve these relationships in the best way possible for each, we should be mainly feeling on a high, as everything we share assists someone else, and ourselves, in ways needed for love, peace, compassion, empathy, etc.

We'll consider a variety of solutions for several love problems:

- Abusive Relationships
- Appreciating each person through their psyches, male/female, and various other combinations
- True feminism
- Empathetic males
- Strong family structures
- Young people's input
- Women and men are people first and ladies and men second
- How can women and men be seen as beautiful creations in the total sense? We need institutions and male/female integrated leadership across the board.

General Solutions

Us Compared to 'Him' – worth a look!!!

Perfection (GOD) vs Non-perfection (Us)

Only one entity in the universe is perfect, and that is the GOD of the world, which has existed and will exist for eternity for all people, ever. When we are told that we are made in the likeness of God, it refers to all those uniquely human qualities which God has given us; these include the ability to Love, forgive, have compassion, etc., to build good friendships and relationships, to be communal and work for each other's well-being, etc. We don't look like God, as we are physical, and God is the absolutely divine/spirit/entity.

But most importantly, to be able to pray to God and build this relationship so that it can be as good as we can make it.

God made each of the billions of people who have been on this earth, are on this earth, or will be on this earth. Each is unique and equally as special to God. God has no favourites. 'He' made them as perfect as He desired. No one is perfect, though, as we all have the Free Will to choose against God, i.e., to sin!

And we all do it, at least sometimes. No one is perfect in any way. Many are close. Even more, try to be. However, as our western world is so very well off compared to the other second and third worlds, our relationship with God is far less than it should be and could be.

We are often the result of everything our world offers, at least for most of us. We seem to lose the need for God! How incredibly selfish is this? To have almost everything distracts us so easily from God.

Who do most people call to when they are in trouble or having serious difficulties, etc.? God!

As soon as people can acknowledge God and God's place in everything, we will begin the quality journey to God. This should always be our primary aim – to search for and find God! Therefore, in the first instance, we only must impress God, not our fellow humanity. We impress God by firstly acknowledging 'His' superiority and leadership over us and then following God's commandments, teachings, and lifestyle out of our Love for God. God's commandments, rules and regulations exist to better us all. When we follow God correctly, great things happen. We even better appreciate what is enormously important in our lives and know what to do. For example, our physical traits do not need repair because God gave each of us what we need appearance-wise in all ways. We must trust in God out of our extreme Love of our God.

Being an imperfect human person is the gift we are. Everyone has imperfections; no matter how hard we try to remove these, some can succeed. We are still imperfect, aiming for legitimate, authentic perfection, as can realistically be attained with our imperfections and faults.

As a population, we certainly waste enormous amounts of money trying to look a certain way, be a particular type of person, have a specific image to maintain, gain various 'bonus points' from those we try to impress, etc.

And all for what?

Forgiveness

Forgiveness is a most challenging process but an essential need within all humans.

People need to forgive others for their wrongdoing towards them. Others need to forgive us for our failings. We need to forgive ourselves. Forgiveness offered and received is essential for the relationship to repair.

Of course, this is not a simple procedure or one with an inevitable outcome. It depends on so much. It depends on our openness to forgive and to be forgiven. It depends on the person we hurt or who hurt us, being open to forgive or being able to accept forgiveness. It sometimes depends on our ability to offer restitution knowingly or unknowingly to the recipient. It depends on our experience of forgiveness and how we have been affected previously. It depends on our personality, mental, physical, and social health, on our standing with the person concerned, and on so much more.

Once we can forgive and be forgiven and affect restitution, if necessary, we are set free. We can live more peaceful, fulfilling lives. Our relationships are more substantial, and we are happier within these. We are more complete as people living in our families, workplaces, communities, etc.

For God believers - We must also appreciate and accept God into our earthly relationships. We need to invite God into our relationships to help strengthen these and be there when difficulties arise. When this happens, God is there to support us and help us work through the challenges until the final loving outcome is achieved.

Primarily, out of love, we are required to place God as the number one in our lives and our relationships. When we can accept this and turn our relationships over to God, we are then open to receiving so much assistance willingly and accept the outcomes as part of God's plan. This is very freeing and something we need to work towards.

Apologising to God for our hurt caused and the wrongdoings done adds another dimension to our improvement and relationship with God. God always wants the best for and of each of us. God knows intrinsically that we will weaken and make mistakes, hurting ourselves and others along the way. We cannot hurt God, but we can freely move away from God through our thoughts and actions. Acknowledging these wrongs and hurts, helps the healing process and brings us closer to our relationship with God. This is God's desire for us.

God loves each of us so much that we all need to be as close as possible to each other and God - in true love.

We acknowledge God as the most awesome, most needed, most rewarding, most loving entity ever in existence. This honesty and need of God will show God the level of our love with 'Him' and each other. The greater our love of God, the greater our existence and closeness to the One and Only God of eternity!!!

We will then become aware of how GOD will Love us in ways we will find incredibly fantastic and necessary. Believing in the awesomeness of God, and living honestly and truthfully with God, allows our love of God and others to come so much to the fore in our relationships.

(Edited Extract from *Where's God? Revelations Today*, 2018, Great Developments Publishers, Gold Coast.)

Forgiveness is Godliness – What do you think?

What is forgiveness? Forgiveness is an essential and critical aspect of Love. Without forgiveness, we can't realign ourselves with the good in ourselves and others.

God=Absolute Love=Absolute Good=Absolute Forgiveness

When we freely and genuinely seek forgiveness from God, others, and ourselves, we are cancelling out the bad and freely recreating the good we have inside - in our true selves.

As humans, our natural desire is for happiness, enjoyment, freedom, success, compassion, empathy, etc. - all critical aspects of genuine love.

It is when we are hurt emotionally, socially, or physically, etc., that we lose sight of our loving relationships for that moment in time. A low point from which we then need to strive to get back on the 'good' track of life. Forgiveness is now essential for this.

We need to forgive others for hurting us. We need others to forgive us for the harm we caused them. We need to forgive ourselves in order to 'clean our slate' - to remove the nastiness or hate etc., we have caused ourselves or others.

Once we have forgiven these various people, including ourselves, we move back closer to each of those concerned. We also move back to God after seeking forgiveness and purity, which is ours genuinely claimed. Once all our sins have been forgiven, we exist in a state of purity (until next, we sin).

Purity should be our aim and desire throughout life. Our purity helps inspire and bring others to be likewise – pure!

God loves each of us so much equally…

We need to be as close as possible

to each other

and God

- in true authentic love.

…**there is no devil as such,**

but there is considerable **evil** throughout this world.

Evil occurs when WE choose to do something against God or God's teachings knowing this to be wrong.

When this occurs, the person is choosing No God to God for that moment in time.

Beautiful Example of Genuine Forgiveness

There are so many beautiful examples of forgiveness, which challenge humanity to do the right thing and forgive others and ourselves. This is dependent on the circumstances but is essential to our healing and that of others.

An excellent example of forgiveness being essential for healing is shown by the beautiful Muslim father who forgave his little son's accidental killer. An absolute inspiration for humanity!

The father of one of the boys killed in the school car crash in Melbourne, Australia, in 2017, offered the ultimate forgiveness to the driver of the car which killed his son in this horrible accidental car crash death.

One of the most challenging aspects of life is forgiving those who have harmed us, especially when harmed beyond imagination.

This is truly a divine act by a loving human being - an absolute lover, believer, and follower of God.

His Islamic faith is giving him incredible strength.

…the beautiful Muslim father who forgave his little son's accidental car crash killer.

An absolute inspiration for humanity!

…His Islamic faith is giving him incredible strength.

Following God Enriches Humanity – Be Truthful and Not Greedy

Why does so much of humanity believe, think, or in their own eyes 'know' that to follow God with any depth is going to take the fun and exhilaration out of life? How could these people be so far from correct? Let's see why.

The familiar feeling is that being a so-called 'goody goody' gets you nowhere. Your life will be dull - so many others will be having fun! There is a so-called human demand for the good people – 'Get a Life'! Especially for those who are religious or have faith in God.

Surely most people don't think that life is fun when they deliberately or accidentally hurt others, or themselves, through their desire to have fun, etc. Good fun is the best fun! Evil fun is just that, evil, which could be at the expense of other people, families, organisations, etc.

God's way is the ideal of fun, rewarding, challenging, but ultimately REAL; don't be fooled any other way.

Look at any of God's messages to us and see if this is so. Let us consider the first couple of Revelations revealed to me in 2016 and written about in *Where's God? Revelations Today* (2018).

1. *Be Truthful.* How can this be considered a negative? Isn't telling the truth a primary belief to benefit us all? Why do we intrinsically dislike liars? Who gains when the truth is told or acted against? Not good people, but those who choose bad! So, to be untruthful is terrible. Someone is hiding something etc., from

135

other/s. Why would a reasonable person hide from the truth? It is to their benefit to be truthful. The untruthful people are harming others and themselves. For what? The greedy selves!

2. *Don't be Greedy*. How can anyone legitimately argue against this? Greed means someone ends up with more than needed, and others have less than required. When this goes to extraordinary amounts of greed, many people are doing without. Often without the necessities for a decent life. Why do certain people aim for this across their lifestyle and existence? Constantly arguing and/or believing that whatever they can get is good for them! Personal and communal greed leads to many people believing that it doesn't matter how much more they can continually gain for themselves, their family, and their associates. For them, it is never enough!

Our lives become enriched by living God's commandments and teachings. Primarily through loving others in whatever form of love depending on the relationship. Following God can only make our lives more fulfilled and rewarding. With the enormous bonus of heading precisely to salvation with God in Heaven.

Gender Solutions

Introduction

If we can keep the keyword, 'RESPECT', at the front and centre of our exploration and discussion on gender solutions, we will have gone quite a way towards solving some often-difficult scenarios we find confront us in life.

When we respect each person, we come across, negative situations should never occur much. Put Love towards all people as the key aim, and we should notice Love will grow for all concerned.

When Love and Respect are our main priorities, bad things shouldn't deliberately happen. Abuse shouldn't occur. Appreciating and respecting the personal psyche should stop any emotional and physical attacks on others. Males should develop their empathetic sides. Families should grow much closer together out of true love. All our feminine sides should develop through these other now positive aspects of life. The equality of all genders put people first. The beauty of each other's true personalities will help lead to integrated and shared leadership, in whatever way honestly treats each person lovingly.

Solutions for the following:

Abuse;
Appreciating differences between male and
female psyche;
Respectful, empathetic males;
Coherent and robust family structure;
True feminism - Women and Men are people
first, female and male second;
How women and men can be seen as beautiful
creations – in the Fullest sense.
Institutions need male/female integrated
leadership.

Abusive Relationships

Every living person on this Earth has the right to be given everything within the system's care to those who need assistance and care according to the human rights and social justice teachings propagated by the United Nations and the various religions. These principles help protect those affected through the injustices, physical, emotional, and/or psychological harm. Abusive treatment is incomprehensible for everyone, no matter the cause or reason! Abusive lifestyles and violent behaviours, physically or emotionally, etc., are historically against the teachings of Jesus and other prophets and religious leaders within most religions worldwide. These include other religious leaders who needed to be able to explain the rights and principles mentioned and to help each escape from the significant effects which they experience.

The abuse of anyone for any reason is absolutely wrong and forbidden, ethically and legally, by the faithful and other members of society and the followers of God worldwide. To even make this statement is beyond the natural and honest situation in which it is given!!! Some secular or religious jurisdictions have little evidence of this within their ethics and laws, yet it is an essential component of life on this Earth.

This often appears in those countries with lower education, wealth, human rights, and social justice issues and principles being accepted and worked towards. Those countries not supporting these rights and principles fully, or indeed only partially, need the remainder of our people worldwide to pressurise these ignorant or deliberately lacking in quality regimes, to come on board and legitimately treat each person within their countries or communities equally as all people need to be treated with uppermost respect.

Yes, people must have the right to choose which of these political and other authoritative choices works best for them. They then must be afforded the fundamental right to choose their direction and philosophy of life, which they believe is best for them, their families and friends, and others within their life cycle and community. And then be able to move towards that free from any fear or favours from anyone.

NO-NO!

NO-NO!

ABUSE!

Appreciating the Basic Difference Between the Female, Male and Others' Psyche.

For many people, if not most, this is often not seen as relatively essential or at all necessary. Its primary tenant is that even though we are all equally responsible for our and other people's security and deserving of our respect equally, some people ignore this. We also need to appreciate slight differences between the genders from both physical and emotional psyche viewpoints.

As we progress through different decades and centuries, particularly our most recent ones, we note a mixture of genders coming to the fore. We now need to appreciate and respect these different genders and how each interrelates with the other and the once accepted standard of male and female partnerships/marriages. Homosexuality has been around for millennia. Each group of different gender, sexuality, and transgender, etc., needs acknowledgement and respect. Just as for all other people, with the freedom to be supported and included comes the necessity to be responsible and loving of all, in whatever way is possible for each person and group.

In general, ladies and girls are more emotionally supportive of others. In comparison, men and boys are more physically and emotionally protective of others. When this and all the other gendered characteristics are working correctly and consistently, various parts of the world often come together as one.

Even though this is the case, all genders need to be aware of each gender's strengths and weaknesses when living through their psyches in ways that benefit each other fully and equally.

Love should be the meeting point between the two great psyches! In general, there are numerous approaches and appreciations of this concept.

Negatively, men can be too physical and try to dominate ladies and girls consciously or subconsciously. This may include violent, disgusting emotional attacks of various levels too. Females may sometimes be too attacking emotionally, trying to destroy or harm other females and males alike through their views and methods.

The worrying statistic here is how physical and emotional violence and abuse seem to increase and not decrease overall, particularly in the 1st world.

Love is real and can set us free when we include it in our lives. When love rules, so do the positive, loving characteristics in most other people around you. People accept this to be a robust and positive reality and work towards it happening regularly within their families and communities.

All genders should be equal in the eyes of the law and ethics worldwide. However, we know of many places worldwide where one gender dominates. These are usually the beliefs of the male groups within those societies (but not always). Each may be religious or not.

When males acknowledge their physical strength as a positive, and women acknowledge their emotional power positively and work on assisting as many people as possible within their spheres of influence, the path to true love is well within reach.

Each gender can help improve the other genders as needed. Some examples of this follow. Men need to accept another depth in their emotional powers and use these to support all others in whatever way is possible, given time, place, and reason. Combining physical strength and emotional strengths helps men become significant influences within their families and communities when used genuinely and responsibly.

Women need to accept males for this, as they help authentic and interested men develop more of their emotional side of life. Women can also increase their emotional characteristics to encourage and support males to use their powers positively to improve all, especially those within loving relationships. The genuine loving and supportive women have incredible positive power in relations, especially in their families and partners/spouses. But all genders need to be open to others as they continue to grow towards a balanced and loving lifestyle. All people are considered equal and never taken advantage of for any reason.

Love is real and can set us free

when we include it in our lives.

When love rules,

so do the positive, loving characteristics

in most people around you.

Respectful, Empathetic Males

Males should try to develop legitimate empathy throughout their lives. Running blind and trying deliberately or not to be the male warrior is both personally limiting and, in many cases, soul-destroying. It is that many of those with this gift show through their experiences.

Other males need to try and develop these empathetic skills and personality strengths. For many, this is quite difficult and, in a considerable number of cases, maybe almost impossible. Yet, they still need to aim for this, firstly, and most importantly, to protect our females from violence and hatred; but also, to assist the males throughout their lifetimes from being rough, vulgar, unfair, and hate-filled. These need to be changed to gentle, generous, fair, and all-around loving.

Ladies and girls need to be allowed to be feminine. Their essential characteristics towards loving, forgiving, sharing, assisting, nurturing, and many more benefit society significantly. If these behaviours and strengths can seriously influence men, then they should, or at least could become more empathetic with and towards the women and girls within their lives.

It has often been the adverse treatment of women by men which has caused so much strife, violence, and abuse towards women. One aspect of this is happening right before our eyes in Afghanistan now at the time of writing this book. The Taliban have taken back over the country due to the invading countries entirely withdrawing their troops and diplomats. These people have proven their beliefs for the ill-treatment and subjugation of women and girls the last time they had power about 20 years ago. History is now repeating itself.

Coherent and Strong Family Structures

The family unit is usually considered the most substantial partnership of all. A strong, loving, supportive, and forgiving family should be the aim of all families worldwide. Through this model, when it is functioning correctly, members of each successfully operating family feel the necessary LOVE, support, forgiveness, and much more.

Each family member needs to play his/her part. Love is the aim – all you must do is operate as loving members of each family and support and encourage one another to show true Love to all. Of course, it won't always be smooth sailing. There will often be conflicts and challenges. Various families will be affected differently. Yet, each person needs to work diligently at it.

This is where Love comes in and helps each person sort out the difficulties. Developing a coherent group will need to accept that a Loving family works hard for resolutions when the wrong or bad happens. The apparent problem is when one or more family members 'fights' against the unit. Not usually violently, yet it may very well be violent. Violence physically and emotionally is illegal, unethical, and could destroy those affected in various ways. Abuse of anyone is evil and disgusting, especially in a family.

Most people operate families well, considering how difficult it sometimes is to do. LOVE is needed to be honest, be understood, and be an active part of all relationships and encounters within each family. Be genuinely sorry when harm to others and harm to yourself occur. Sort it out through forgiving each other as quickly as possible and getting on with life in a positive way.

True Feminism

True feminism is true equality for all females and males together. No gender is more superior to the other in whatever lifestyle is led, whatever beliefs are espoused. Whatever ethical framework works best for each person within whatever group of people operates together needs to be the aim.

Usually, the men have the power and control over the women in most life activities, etc. Even though this is the traditional, historical outcome, it is not correct practice, particularly in today's developed world. Women should have equal power with men whenever possible. Allowing for the different skills, personalities, powers, and influence each has should develop positive roles for each gender, etc.

Sometimes this doesn't work because the situation doesn't allow it to work fully. Often the argument is that the women aren't as experienced or qualified as the men in the workplace due to time off for their children. Indeed, the best person, male or female, for a particular position is the ideal, to keep the organisation or industry, etc., in proper and fair competition with others in their fields. This should mean that overall lifestyles, industries, vocations, etc., encourage a balance works out.

The ideal is that out of LOVE, each gender works towards peace, harmony, and Love, equally between each person, no matter their gender or any other discriminatory possibility. This also challenges many people who believe that they are better at whatever they are doing than their competitors and cannot accept that everyone else is equal. Everyone is human. Every human is similar to all others. Females and males are equal as people. Yet, they have different abilities and experiences, which impact their places within our world. True feminism helps build a more vital, more loving world of equality between females and males.

The ideal is that out of LOVE,

each gender works towards peace, harmony, and Love,

equally between each person,

no matter their gender or any other discriminatory possibility...

Females and males are equal as people.

Yet, they have different abilities and experiences, which impact their places within our world.

True feminism lived by females and males

helps considerably build a more vital, more loving world of equality between females and males

and other human sexualities and genders.

Women, Men and Others are People First and Female, Male and Others Second

A most beautiful experience is to realise for the first time that women are truly equal to men. And men not being superior in any balanced way. Each gender has its strengths. We need to realise that all people have so much to offer our world, no matter their gender. To learn that through our gender differences, we are made whole as a people.

It is essential to realise that there is much more to a person than their gender. There is a real need here to not see them in a sexual way but to see them first as a person, a fully-fledged human being. Their sexuality is so fundamental. It is crucial to delineate between their sex appeal and their sexuality (being feminine or masculine, etc.). Emphasizing the feminine and masculine aspects of people will allow the freedom to see each as a genuinely liberated human.

As a male, it saddens me that it appears that most of society does not feel this way and never has. There are so many reasons why including, including:

a. not accepting that you can separate the sexual aspect from the sexuality aspect,
b. an unstated feeling of inadequacy by males,
c. the threat of the unknown,
d. the way culture has always been historical,
e. some women and men do not support this belief,
f. the fundamental premise that that is just the way it is! etc.
g. the growing appreciation of other 'genders' apart from male and female, e.g., transgender people.

It is essential to acknowledge the solid feminine characteristics and how these make a woman exceptional and equal. These characteristics include: to be compassionate, caring, nurturing, be gentle, and loving in a feminine way. And yes, individual males and females indeed have these characteristics in varying degrees. Yet, a woman, in general, has these to a greater degree. That is not wrong or bad. It is good and helps our lifestyles and beliefs. It adds depth to the general male and female genders and the strengths each carries through their relationships. The binary genders have existed forever. Males used only to marry females, and in most cases, incredible results happen. Same-sex marriage now exists in many countries.

Interestingly, it is felt that men can develop these feminine characteristics to a high degree. When a male is enculturated within this belief, surrounded by like-minded people, invited extrinsically or intrinsically to become a valued participant, then it is believed he more than likely will accept such a situation. He will then begin to develop his feminine side. And likewise for ladies and girls. With life experiences and challenges, each will create their feminine and masculine sides. Once this development starts, it is tough to stop because the reality of women and men being equal becomes so true to him.

We can operate in a way where female and male characteristics are not a threat but an enhanced aspect of everyone's life. We are on our way to a far better world. This should be a world of less stress, a world of more hope, a world of greater love, where more equality and respect are shared between people male and female and other genders alike.

How Can Women, Men and Others Be Seen as Beautiful Creations – in the Fullest Sense?

Women, men and other genders are such beautiful creations in the most fundamental and whole sense. They are much more than physical, sexual beings. They are a complete package of the physical, emotional, intellectual, social, sexual, and spiritual.

Yet, why are women and other genders, excluding males, most often diminished in society? They are usually not given the opportunities of men, not respected as much as men, and not seen as equal to men in every way. Countries and cultures vary here.

These perceptions must not be allowed. Society must actively teach the respect and equality of both women and men and other sexualities.

How can people reach such a liberating belief and see people as beautiful creations? Some topics worth exploring include:

a. Leaders need to lead positively, reasonably and to encourage all people to achieve in ways that benefit others, not allowing for any resultant harm.
b. There is a need to be open-minded to the goodness in all people.
c. No matter a person's gender, if a person feels valued and respected, then this goodness will blossom.
d. Drop the stereotypes – the historical role and place of women and men in society. Unless both parties agree on specific lifestyle plans equally, both would most desire these to be a significant part of their lives together.

e. Often, we need to change our priorities and values as the world and we change throughout our lives.

f. Accept people for who they no matter their gender, race, colour, religion, etc.

g. Allow for unconditional love.

Once women feel entirely accepted by both men and other women alike, they will feel truly free to be themselves. Their inner and outer beauty will radiate and positively impact those around them, often creating a domino effect. Society will be empowered with those beautiful and incredible characteristics often lacking when both men and women are not acting as a whole.

Nothing is more beautiful than people who genuinely value each other working and living together with a common cause. Success will follow if we can encourage people to stop the negatives, especially greed and jealousy, and take on those of true love for all. This can be a reality but needs people to accept and value others initially.

Eventually, when people are sincere and truthful in their relationships, the beautiful, loving creations of both women and men will develop into a new, most inspiring paradigm: one where each person, male, female and other, will grow to reach their full Loving potential. This will be where each person will be happy and content with their lot. The expression of what each person truly desires, i.e. true love here on Earth, will be the leading personal aim. Yes, some may argue that this is only a state of idealism. Yet, the reality is attainable when people develop their weaknesses into strengths and continue developing their strengths higher.

Eventually, when people are sincere, truthful and
Loving in their relationships,
the beautiful, loving creations of both
women and men
will develop into a new, most inspiring paradigm:
one where each person,
male, female, and others,
will grow to reach their full Loving potential.

Institutions and Male/Female Integrated Leadership

Institutions need to wake up to the power of integrated leadership and workforce membership. To be places where all people feel truly valued and are fully respected for who they are and what they can offer and not what their gender may be.

Unfortunately, there is such an overwhelming paradigm shift needed before this can become the norm. Women need to be accepted as equal to men in all ways. Yes, with different yet complementary traits, which help make the whole so enabling.

How successful are our institutions in enabling this change? From the beginning, are parents treating each gender truly equally. Are single-sex schools educating for equality? Are co-educational schools any better? Are employers encouraging all their employees to aim for greatness within their industries, be the best they can be whatever their roles, and select the best people for their middle and senior leadership positions? Religious, community, sporting, and cultural organisations show that each person is equal through their policies and practices. Opportunities for success and leadership must be equally offered, depending on ability at each challenge?

What hope do we ever have of true gender equality and leadership being met?

We need to ask honestly, is it that important that we do everything we can to commercially consume as much as possible, gain that better position, better pay rise or more improved status, etc.? If positive relationships and true love are our intrinsic goals in life, then are rampant consumerism, high wealth, and dog-eat-dog mentality going to benefit anyone?

We all know of people who are nasty, manipulative and self-seeking, etc. Even these people should change when surrounded by both an authentically loving, caring community and workforce, etc.

Leadership is critical for success. Leaders and the general population need to show the true values that attract Love. They need to show that self-aggrandisement, greed, lording power over others, and selfishness, etc., which leads to others' insecurities, lack of esteem, and rejection, is not worth the effort – and is incorrect. Better results come for all when the whole and each individual is considered as valued.

Ambition and drive are often crucial for many people's and organisations' success, yet these need not be negative. When these operate for the betterment of others and the organisation, all win.

We need to ask ourselves, what really will make us happy seriously? When it comes to the crunch, most people will be satisfied by just attaining what they need. This would be gained ethically. When this is done Lovingly, it will lead to a more cohesive and productive society. It will be a society where both women and men are genuinely valued for who they are and what they can offer the whole.

If positive relationships and true Love are our basic goals in life,

then are rampant consumerism, high wealth, and dog-eat-dog mentality going to benefit anyone?

A Nation's First People, e.g., 'Australian Aborigines'

Indigenous On the Road to Liberation - Wujal Wujal Aboriginal Community FNQ

Visiting one of our first people's communities was an extraordinary experience. As part of our road trip north, my wife and I stopped at the Wujal Wujal first people's community on the northern edge of the Daintree National Park in Far North Queensland (FNQ), Australia. It took quite an effort getting here over many kilometres of gravel, unsealed roads, creeks, being many kilometres from the next major frontier town of Cooktown.

We found an alcohol-free community of 360 people working to become one with the 21st century. There was a store, a community building, many houses of a good standard, a football field and a baseball field (up the road a little), a new business complex comprising a café, an art gallery (with most items in stock for sale) and a community art workshop. There was also a primary school and kindergarten.

There was a generally pleasant feel around the small town - we drove around the streets. Most houses and yards were quite well kept, clean and tidy, yet with the regulation minor town flaws, few of which were overrun with grass, weed, or disposed of goods. Many children were around due to this being the winter school holidays.

The locals were happy to wave in response to our gesture - this added to the pleasant feel and 'welcoming' to their town.

The typically 'accepted' stereotypes expected of these towns were not visible. A peaceful tranquillity was evident. There were no drunks, no loud, uncontrollable noise, no dirty, unkept people or places. It was a community worth exploring further.

A newly constructed building has been built next to the bridge where people travelling south first enter the Daintree National Park. It is well-positioned to attract attention, and hopefully, much business. The building comprises a café, an art gallery, and a community art workshop.

This newly established business by the Wujal Wujal Aboriginal Shire Council aims to be both a training facility for the local people and a successful business venture. Young people worked and trained in the hospitality field within the art gallery and café. A couple of non-indigenous ladies held the critical roles of manager, supervisor, and senior trainer. Yet, this could change when the younger ones gain experience?

According to the Council's website (See details at the end of this article), there is also a women's centre, a radio training facility for certificate 3 and 4 qualifications, a library (Indigenous Knowledge Centre), a part-time bank/post office, and a sports building. Tours are run into the Daintree.

Allowing for the people's generally quiet and often shy nature and cultural mores, there was much to admire about these indigenous first Australians. It appeared that they were trying to meet both the needs of their culture, as well as the culture to which they want to be an accepted part.

However, there was also what appeared to be a limited amount of opportunity for the locals if they wished to pursue other careers. There was little else that was apparent to do beyond these ventures. Apart from the noticeable number of people interested in fishing, including the rather elderly man spearfishing, it seemed that the people had to leave this community if they wished to pursue other careers. This seemed very unfortunate, as it would lessen the community and family life. However, there may be enough to do around the neighbourhood to sustain it, and I won't propose to be informed otherwise.

Facilities need to be developed further, which will provide enjoyable, fun, cultural activities, sporting activities, and various business and career opportunities, etc.

It seems that there may be not enough happening to sustain a balanced, family and community-friendly town.

This community is trying very hard to make its existence beneficial. The Queensland government had taken away the alcohol ten years ago. Still, it hadn't added enough activities and interests for these people in the town to engage all the locals fully. It seems to us to be a situation where the taking away of accepted Australian freedom to drink alcohol responsibly has not been replaced, or supported, anywhere near enough.

We would have trouble being an active member of this community, bearing in mind what we, like Australians in general, accept as the norm of any society. More positive discrimination needs to be done by the powers so that equality with mainstream Australia may one day be present in the Wujal Wujal township.

(http://www.wujalwujalcouncil.qld.gov.au/)

Hopelessness - Outback - First People's Towns - More Solutions Need True Love

When does something fundamental become so hopeless that it will never be able to be hoped for again? Of course, Never!

How does such a lack of Love become positive and loving for all? Hopelessness needs to get solved or redirected to successfully shared and open endeavours for all local people in each town? This is often the case worldwide for each country's first people.

Love starts in the homes and families. Children and adults need to show love for all people who live within their homes. These also need to be displayed within the community on a day-to-day basis. When people feel truly loved, they can do much more for themselves and others. You can feel these disadvantaged people calling out for guidance, example, and support by their leaders or from others they love and invite to help them through the challenges.

The historical media coverage of the hopeless aboriginal lifestyle situation in Tennant Creek, NT, Australia, reminds me of our time travelling through there and many other predominantly aboriginal towns on our trip up the Stuart Highway from Adelaide to Darwin. And across to Kununurra in WA.

There was an absolute sense of hopelessness and deprivation in most outback towns. (Yet, Wujul Wujul, near the Daintree in north Queensland, seemed to be or becoming, a much better led and lived town.)

Reasons:

Most often, the overriding reason is a lack of worthwhile and liberating work, along with other helpful social engagement facilities within the community! It is so obvious, yet what is being done in the field to solve it? Once there are worthwhile employment and positive social endeavours available and an improvement in local indigenous health and welfare, especially with positive mental health and self-worth, many of the other inherent problems within aboriginal communities will be on the way to a solution.

The clear view of many Aussies is that the indigenous do not want to work. I don't believe this, and statistically, it isn't so. Of course, in any society, some would rather live an alternative lifestyle. Many have never had the opportunity to work where enjoyment, passion, and a real sense of pride and place within the community abounds. Most towns don't have anywhere near enough enhancing employment opportunities or community-engaging activities.

One solution:

Kununurra in far north-eastern Western Australia is one example where many first peoples have chosen a particular lifestyle that suits their needs and helps lead to positivity. A former aboriginal liaison officer for one of the mines explained that the first peoples often have a different attitude to work than the standard western view. Many of these locals prefer to work for months or a few years and then take time off and live off their earnings while being one with their country and a more relaxed, traditional lifestyle. They would then return to work when additional income was needed. They enjoy this option.

Bryan Foster

Tennant Creek, NT, Major Issues:

The Tennant Creek social situation has become so bad that it has taken years of sexual and physical abuse reporting, hundreds of underage STI reports, and a recent two-year old's rape to start things moving. Imagine if this abuse were happening in eastern Australia specifically and not the desert towns.? The outcry would be incredible, just as the outcry was when ABC's Four Corners showed the Don Dale Detention Centre abuse. It led to a Royal Commission being implemented from the next day after going to air. After various legal manoeuvres and commission involvement, a class action has been won by these young offenders, who were treated exceptionally poorly as inmates. Plus, the youth's detention centre and NT's totally out of proportion number of inmates/young aboriginal people compared to the non-indigenous peoples of the Northern Territory. This is a relatively new sort of outcome for young people. Television and newspapers (Murdock's mainly) basically lead the way for this result to become real.

Statistically, the situation doesn't appear to be bad at all. (See the last paragraph.) It is only when you scratch the surface that the issues become apparent. Thank you, ABC television and Murdoch press, for researching and reporting this.

But the problem at Tennant Creek is so entrenched that no one seems capable of solving it. There were limited reactions from senior politicians. Initially, there was no serious response from any governmental leader in the NT. No real aboriginal leadership outcry for assistance and training, etc., so as to become genuine township leaders, etc., except a few aboriginal leadership people. Aboriginal people will tell of the difficulty of getting local people and political leaders together to help solve all these major problems. The indigenous people of all countries need the primary say in their lifestyle choices. Other nationalities need involvement so as to use the best minds available to work together to solve such major problems of the local first peoples. If the ABC and 'The Australian' newspaper hadn't alerted us to the problems, it would still be a 'nasty secret' of outback NT, Australia - at two different places (so far???) Tennant Creek and the Don Dale Detention Centre.

Tennant Creek finally got a large amount of money from all levels of government, federal, state and local council, to help with their town's challenges and needs. This $80m aid package is being used to lift all the township's standards of life, work, health, education, socialisation, etc. Yet, many appear to not be happy with various spending choices and decisions. (See this news article link for details – (**Tennant Creek Aboriginal leaders say $80 million aid package prompted by toddler's rape being misdirected - ABC News**)

Statistics:

If the billions that have been wasted over the decades had gone into decent, life-enhancing job creation ventures, social enhancement projects, and drug and alcohol educational and health programs, all with significant aboriginal community input and leadership, the next future billions spent would have been considerably less and more specifically directed to the necessary need of the first peoples.

The statistics for Tenant Creek are pretty surprising. Much analysis is required. Some statistics which stand out: Aborigine to non-aborigine is almost 50/50, over 80% have less than a diploma's education, the median age is 33, around 2.5 times fewer people are over 70 years, and there are twice as many communities and personal service workers proportionately to the rest of Australia, almost 40% single-parent families to the rest of Australia and double the rental accommodation to Australia overall.

Extrapolating for aborigines, Tennant Creek is approximately 50% aboriginal, who are educated mainly to year 10 level or a TAFE certificate 3 level, with a young median age of 33 and a high proportion of single parents 40%, all who live in twice as many rental properties to the rest of Australia and who have access to twice as many community and personal workers proportionately. (Source ABS below.)

Solutions (some):

Aboriginal guided and eventually led:

- Life-enhancing, worthwhile job creation ventures and employee training.
- social enhancement projects.
- functional downtime facilities and activities.
- drug and alcohol educational and health programs, which are accepted by the needy.
- isolation ridding programs, including quality internet and improved communications.
- local media posts, e.g., radio, television, and streaming – to run good news stories, news, educational programs, documentaries, general entertainment, and sport. The high content of local aborigines employed. Streamed or broadcast over the airwaves.
- positive, life-filled, and loving community.

Expertise from the broader Australian community will be needed to assist in these developments. This outside expertise would need to be continually monitored until the local aborigines can, where possible, fully control and run each enterprise. The timelines for withdrawal would vary depending on familiarity and expertise, size, complexity, etc. And leadership from both non-indigenous experts in these fields, along with supportive aboriginal leadership and drive.

There will also be options for local non-indigenous and outsiders to form joint ventures with the local indigenous. These would need to be created so that the outsiders would respect the locals and their needs and input and never be allowed to take over the business. These businesses should all be owned and operated by the local first peoples. This may include others who are not original inhabitants, yet in a minor way so that the aboriginal people have total control, as well as organisation, and gain from these skills and experiences.

Tennant Creek is the prominent example used. There are so many other outback towns in similar or far worse situations. All need both the local and broader communities to stand up and demand proper research and exposure of the problems. To then work with the local aboriginal community actively towards solutions. Way too much money has been wasted over the decades. Time to genuinely listen to the local first people on the ground and become money smart, investing in worthwhile endeavours while still assisting the local indigenous get through some challenging lifestyle experiences until they are ready to lead for themselves.

ABS (Australian Bureau of Statistics) Detailed Statistics:

Tennant Creek statistically from the ABS for 2016 (Sometimes rounded off %): 51% aborigine, 70% f/t work and of these 75% work over 35 hrs/week, 18% have diploma or higher, median age is 33, 4% are 70 or older (10.7 Aust.), no religion 34%, unemployed 7.1% (6.9% Aust), Community and Personal Service Workers 20.3% (10.8% Aust), Income $650 ($662 Aust), one parent families 22% (16% Aust), 30% unoccupied dwellings (11% Aust), 64% rented (31% Aust), Single person households 33% (24% Aust), medium rent $175 ($335 Aust), Internet dwellings 69% (83% Aust), medium rent at least 1 person aboriginal $150 ($250 Aust)

The overriding reason is a lack of worthwhile and liberating work, along with other helpful social engagement facilities within the community!

It is so obvious, yet what is being done in the field to solve it? First people's involvement is critical to success.

Once there are worthwhile employment and positive social endeavours available and an improvement in local indigenous health and welfare, especially with positive mental health and self-worth, many of the other inherent problems within aboriginal communities will be on the way to a solution.

Reflecting on a Country's Day, Starts with the Country's First People's

Our country. The land and its people, us. It is from the ground that all life begins, grows, and dies. Our lives are nourished, challenged, and taken by the country. We need to Love our countries, wherever these are. That is good for our lives! Love life!

The Australian land is divine for me. It is ultimately in and through the land that I indeed find God. People with the country at heart echo and live God's calling for us all. They are the sunrise, the highest peaks, and the refreshing cool waters. They hold solutions for floods, droughts, bushfires, and other natural disasters.

So many of us love this sunburnt country absolutely to the core.

Celebrate Australia Day for what Australia is, stands for, and tries to encompass. Allow for past pains and present flaws because, at our core, we are good people with good intentions. Allow for errors and mistakes trying to be rectified; that's Australian.

Personally, my ancestry is primarily British and French. It probably also includes some Australian aboriginal lineage from Tasmania. Yet to be confirmed.

The genuineness of all people who follow the Australian values will need to continue their fight for equality. The rich, talented, and gifted in all fields will need to share more. The poor and suffering will be opened to receiving assistance, education, health, and opportunities.

Bryan Foster

Dorothea Mackellar's 'My Country' says it all. She wrote it at the beginning of the 20th century by a third-generation Australian missing Australia while travelling to England. The poem highlights so much of 'her beauty and her terror [Australia's]'.

MUST SEE the moving, heart-felt video of the 'My Country' song by 18 years old Christine Roberts published and sung in 1967 and released on CBS. Includes artworks by famous Australian artist Russell Drysdale. Along with a short backstory interview with Dorothea Mackellar by Christine just before her death.

'I love a sunburnt country,
A land of sweeping plains,
Of ragged mountain ranges,
Of droughts and flooding rains.
I love her far horizons,
I love her jewel-sea,
Her beauty and her terror
The wide brown land for me!' (Extract from 'My Country')

http://www.censusdata.abs.gov.au/census_services/getprod uct/census/2016/quickstat/SSC70251

Tennant Creek - Drive Through video by Bryan Foster: https://www.youtube.com/watch?v=PNsop7an73I

Tennant Creek Aboriginal leaders say $80 million aid package prompted by toddler's rape being misdirected - ABC News

http://www.dorotheamackellar.com.au/archive/mycountry.h tm   Christine   Roberts'   (1967)   song: http://splash.abc.net.au/home#!/media/104826/?id=10482 6

Love is the Meaning of Life

Introduction to Love is the Meaning of Life

Love is the Meaning of Life for so many people historically and presently - i.e. The meaning of life is Love. We could also safely add the billions of people still to be born. Love adds that incredible depth to so many relationships. To be in Love can occur on so many levels. In this section of the book, we will highlight some of the many aspects of Love through the themes below. There is a mixture of positive and negative impacts on us through our Love. These author articles were created over the past decade+ and are updated now.

Why do We Want to Live a Full Life so Strongly?
But – Life's Not Fair
You Can't Have Everything
All are Equal in God's Eyes
Our Divine Eyes
The Solution is Love
Forgiveness
Moonbeam Capture
Love can't be found on the computer screen, even less in the smartphone – just look skyward
Music and Song - Fantastic Inspiration for True Love: Leonard Cohen (dec.), Elvis Presley (dec.), Leo Downey - Musicians for God
Leo Downey
Social Justice Principles and Human Rights
Perfection – Being Physically Perfect! Why?
Secularism is Dangerous and Hollow
Secularism is Leading Humanity to a Catastrophe
Heretic by Aayan Ali

Why do We want to LIVE a FULL LIFE so Strongly?!

That sounds like a dumb question, do you think???

Why do humans want to live so long and not die? Especially when the faithful appreciate what it is like being with God in Heaven. If we know this and desire to know the answers, we are growing closer to God and becoming One with the Absolute Love and being encased fully in LOVE - Forever! (However, it is a typical secular belief that life is over and totally extinguished at death? Some may have less doubt and are still exploring the options.)

The older we get, the more appreciative of our lives we seem to get. The more we appreciate every single day! We know we live on a knife's edge, and anything can happen to us at any time. The world is full of accidents, illnesses, and natural and human-made catastrophes, and so much more, all of which could end our lives in a second!

Most people by 50 to 60 years of age will have had a few very close encounters where life could be death in a split second. A couple of mine come to mind quite quickly. The time I was surfing as a seventeen-year-old during a building cyclonic surf and was thrown off the surf ski while at the top of a massive breaking wave and ended up smashed in turbulent waters where I could not see where I was and didn't know up from down. I survived and wondered how and why. Another time was when a bus in Paris almost collected me while I was about to cross a pedestrian crossing. I literally almost became a death statistic from being hit by a bus!!! It didn't stop at the traffic lights.

The more I reflect and interact with nature and goodness and love within our world, the more I love it, and the more robust this love becomes, especially over time. Yet, many know that Heaven will be so much more. Being unable to fathom this at any depth, though, due to our humanity and all its limitations, helps us desire our world in a very positive yet limiting way.

God obviously wants us to enjoy the world 'He' deliberately created for us; otherwise, why create this and share it with us all? Why guide us, mainly through scripture and prayer, etc., on how to be stewards of creation for all time.

God wants us to develop our LOVE of people and nature and make each person's life on earth unique and special. We can't understand why, except it is out of God's Absolute Love for all creation that it comes, created, and shared with us fully!

Some see it as a trial to see if we are worthy of salvation in Heaven. Others see it as task-driven to develop all those necessary skills needed to make the world a fair and just place for all creation. Etc. Heaven is for the perfect (as much as possible) human beings. This next point will probably challenge many people, yet it has been discerned as from God over many years - I also believe it is for all plants (flora) and animals (fauna) whose souls have developed as close as possible to God. Souls=Life (for all living creations). Not just humans!

Others who take the negative route and believe there is no salvation and/or no God often lead challenging lives, quite lost in aim and directions. Therefore, greed and lust and most things negative become a significant aim of their lives. Many believe that because in their eyes this is the only life and nobody else cares for you, that you should take as much as you can from it and enjoy it yourself or with your loved ones. Wrong!

God needs us to choose love over hate, life over death, joy over sorrow, etc. - until that moment in time when God calls us home to Heaven. This is where we started and the primary option for ending after death. Evil ones who deliberately choose evil beliefs and lifestyles and reject God and God's absolute Love fail to seek forgiveness of God for their evil, sinful ways and then end up in an eternity of evil.

Hence, the reason we want to live a fulfilled life comes from God out of God's Absolute Love and desire for our best. Generally, we have an intrinsic feel for this Love and these beliefs - and desire it strongly before moving on to God at death!

…the reason we want to live a fulfilled life comes from God out of God's ABSOLUTE LOVE and desire for our best.

However, we cannot properly appreciate this,

as it comes from divinity, God,

and we only have our humanity to embrace and understand it as best we can.

Generally, we have an intrinsic feel for this love and these beliefs - and desire it strongly before moving on to God at death!

But - Life's Not Fair – Where's the Love?

Life is not fair, even with all the Love that exists within each person and the world as a whole. Life indeed isn't fair in the sense we commonly use it. But…

It is straightforward to sit back in a first world country and complain about how tough life is. Maybe we could spend some time in a third-world country living their lifestyle on their means and then ask how fair life is. Many in third world countries could do likewise in their own countries and see others worse off than themselves.

Life's fairness is so relative.

We all expect the best for ourselves and our loved ones. We would probably go to exceptional lengths to make this occur. And in many cases, they already do.

How can we legitimately complain about fairness when billions are far worse off?

What is fairness anyway? Is it equality of wealth and opportunities? Is it empathy for all fellow humans? Is it social justice for all? Is it all these and more?

Even in countries with virtually everything needed, such as in many western countries - life is not fair. Even when the great majority of these people stand up for their justice system, health and education systems, social services and welfare systems, police and security systems, wage system, and freedoms beyond so many other countries, there is still an avalanche of social injustice. Add to this the egalitarianism, equality, and opportunities for all found in a few countries, and there are still various problems of fairness remaining.

Someone born into a wealthy, educated, informed, and powerful family is far more likely to have a comfortable life; to have so many life and career opportunities. To have the chance to marry into other wealthy, influential families. To have so much that their understanding of the poor is compromised chiefly to support their elitist regime.

The view that some have this or that because of hard work and that those others who don't have the essentials can only blame themselves for their problems is mostly wrong. It is hard to argue that people want similar things, yet life's choices or inevitabilities end up differently for each person. Those fortunate enough to gain more often don't want to share much of it, while those who ended up with less would like the others to share. This argument is based on where a person stands on the wealth continuum. Unfair for the poor! Not fair for the wealthy - who have so much more and don't need anything like what they have.

Unfortunately, most rich people think the poor control their lives. They use this to justify doing no more for them than necessary. It allows these people with so much to sleep comfortably, guilt-free. Who would choose poverty and deprivation over wealth and power? Who would not choose motivated, successful parents, family, and friends to guide and shape their every move and development and literally be role models of the wealthy? Who would not choose a good education at a good school followed by an excellent tertiary qualification? And the choices go on…

Fairness is about so many aspects of life, not just money. We need to consider all elements associated with a population's health, education, career opportunities and enhancements, societal relationships, equality before the law, access to adequate housing, clothing, temperature control, pollution control, and other environmental effects on people. In fact, in all aspects of life, that impact and affect each person. It is also a significant amount more than just looking after culture, nation, community or religious group, etc. It is totally about looking after each within their community.

Is GOD unfair to people? NO!!!

People choose to be unfair to each other out of their God-given Free Will.

Overall, life is fair in the sense that our lives are God-given for us to do as we find possible and loving. To do to others and the whole creation as we find possible and loving. The fairness begins with us reaching the age of reason, around 7-9 years of age. In God's eyes, life is fair as we are created equal and placed in this world together. Of course, there is an aspect of mystery, e.g., why were we placed where and when we were and in our circumstances? People (not God) take the fairness out of life – primarily due to greed, the second Revelation given by God to me (and possibly others worldwide) in May 2016 – 'Don't Be Greedy'.

We all know what needs to be done, but how many do the hard things? The strict sharing, caring, equalising things needed for fairness worldwide? The fundamental, life-saving, empathetic, loving necessities all people need to do and accept.

If people were sincere (the First Revelation from God in May 2016 was - Be truthful), they would accept that they are greedy, placing themselves first and others down the line as a generalisation. Most wouldn't see it this way and would probably argue against it. Why? For the unfair people, it's easier to deny than accept. To accept will likely mean a significant life change for the rich, who many would consider, by far, don't care too much about the poor in general overall; unless the poor and disadvantaged impact upon them in such a way as to affect their lifestyles, careers, wealth, powers, etc.

Here's the big question. When was the last time you split your assets with others so that each person could live a fair and just existence?

God must allow all our choices to occur because we have been given absolute freedom out of God's unlimited love for us to choose God's way through our informed conscience or the other way. Because God loves us absolutely, we have to have total freedom to choose from God or evil. We have been given the rules and guidelines on living successful, rewarding lives for all. Fairness dictates that we must choose God! If not, evil would be untruthful and greedy.

No, life's not fair anywhere!

Greed rules. Privilege rules. Power and money talk!

The most disappointing reality to all of this is that there are enough resources worldwide for all people to live genuine, comfortable lives Everywhere. But all people have to share their excesses. Excesses are resources beyond the necessities. All people need to be Truly generous and loving, and empathetic. Most people could share their excesses, yet how many could share a more realistic, more generous amount to give the poor a good, loving life?

Unfortunately, we all know this will probably never happen, as stated above. People's nature, nationalism, greed, and generally speaking a genuine dislike by the haves with helping the huge majority of others, the have-nots. But many of humanity are forever hopeful that this will occur in our lifetimes.

Can it start? Yes. Can it happen to a degree? Yes. It's up to us to do our own thing to help, financially, politically, socially, etc. Give it a go! You won't know how good it is until you are a part of what should be a massive movement – eventually!

GOD loves all people equally and needs us to do likewise. To give everyone a fair go. So that life can be fair when we all work together to find true Love!

It is from this place onwards that fairness begins to disappear, mainly due to humanity's choices. Sometimes it could be due to the fate of natural events beyond our control - part of the mystery of GOD and what GOD places before each of us.

The most disappointing reality to all of this
is that there are enough resources worldwide
for all people to live genuine, comfortable lives
everywhere.

But all people must at least share their excesses.

Excesses are resources beyond the necessities.

All people need to be Truly generous, loving, and
empathetic.

You Can't Have Everything

It seems such an obvious statement, yet so many these days believe they can have, be, do everything they so desire! They lose any sense of realism by being caught up with so much marketing and well-being, goal setting, dreaming hype. Aiming to be our realistic best is crucial. It is so much a less stressful, rewarding, self-fulfilled lifestyle when one accepts that there will be limitations, unbeatable challenges, fewer opportunities than expected. To not always want and need more than is realistically possible or even desirable is liberating. Being honest is real!

The notion that if I dream it and want it badly enough and seriously work towards it, then it WILL become real is often so off the mark. Just ask some challenging questions, e.g., could the author ever become an astronaut at my age – answer no. No matter what I dream, work towards, want, 'need', this can never happen. Why? Primarily because of my age and health! Probably also because I would not be able to gain the proper training required, etc. You might argue, well it is different for young people. Yes, for some, but not for most. If you don't have the academic, intellectual, physical, and emotional characteristics needed for such an endeavour, it doesn't matter how much dreaming, working hard, and dedication you aim for; it just can't happen. It is also the case for many other career moves. How many young people believe they are being belittled, not yet being their company's 'go-to' person? How many don't think you have to start at an appropriate level, which isn't a manager or CEO?

The young, and many not so young, are facing such strong family and significant adult support and developing a sense of entitlement well beyond reality. Too many helicopter parents do so much for their children that they miss the opportunities to work hard, make mistakes, take responsibility for their actions, and become better people. Too many adults want their children to be so 'successful' that they don't give them the foundations needed to achieve success in its truest sense.

People need to have dreams, goals, and hope for future 'prosperity and success', realistically - Aim high. Work hard. Be the best you can be. But be real. Realise that there are limitations and a lack of opportunities. But always be on the lookout and be ready for the good options when these come. But always be aware of what makes you truly happy and content. Excesses don't do this! Materialism and excessive power, don't do this.

Good people who genuinely care about you and your well-being will be your authentic support. Be on the lookout for those who want excesses for themselves and you. Do they know what is best for themselves? For you? Or are they also trapped in the unreality of excess and other associated unrealistic expectations?

God is our best guide and support. Keep in contact with God, primarily through prayer, and be aware of what God wants for you. God has a plan for each of us. Keep doing what you inherently feel is right, comforting, personally rewarding, and best for you as an individual and as an essential family and community member.

We need to ask God to help us, support us and bring us peace and prosperity in its truest sense. Remember that God wants the best for you and is always there for you. Just ask. We were created to be the best we can become.

No two of us are the same.

When we open ourselves to what God wants for us and go along with it, there develops a real, authentic, comforting sense of peace and fulfilment.

You become one with God in this world.

All People are Equal in 'God's Eyes'

All are created equal and should have similar quality lifestyles, no matter the prevailing political system, culture, or religion in operation.

God has no favourites. Everyone is equal. Every single creation is perfect in God's eyes. Each person needs to have all the same rights and privileges. There are no exceptions for any reason! To believe otherwise breaks God's teachings and commandments.

These divine messages are simple. God is absolutely fantastic beyond belief and needs to be seen, respected, and treated as such by all people. All people need to be treated equally by each other, just as God treats them equally.

When it comes to those who aren't treated this way, God acts and tells us to do likewise. God is especially with and in the poor, destitute, and disadvantaged. Apart from loving each of us equally, another reason is so that their lives can be equalised to be like others. There needs to be a massive positive change in this world for people to be equal - in all countries, cultures, religions, and groups.

Why do most adolescents (teens to 20s) favour social justice for all? Why do they seek a noble cause and then fight for this with a passion? Why is this trait so inherent in people? It is often attained even when parents actively do everything in their power to stop it. It becomes a matter for the haves to fight so hard for their advantages. How could any wealthy person live a happy, successful life with just the basics? Easily - especially when everyone is doing the same and being as FAIR as possible!

Our Divine Eyes

Nothing is more beautiful than our divine eyes! Nothing allows a vision of the true humanity of someone more than through these. The eyes say it all! The eyes are indeed the window to a person's soul. To the authentic self. To our oneness with God.

Through the eyes is where you get to see where someone is. It is exceedingly difficult, if not impossible, for someone to fake their eyes and the messages they are sending through these. The overall appearance, the use of the eyelids, surrounding frowns, smiles, etc., can change and be acted differently, giving a different message. The overall facial appearance may be real or fake. The visible eyes, including the iris and pupil, are the conduit to the true self.

Through the eyes, we sense where and when the person is genuine and authentic, truthful, and loving. There is a God-given depth seen through the eyes. The more open, loving, and egalitarian a person, the more viewed 'within' through the eyes.

The eyes' irises are also a most beautiful aspect of each person's physical self. These encompass their physical colourings and intimate aspects of personal characteristics, including speckles, colour variations, and other intricate designs.

Loving, genuine, authentic people shine through their eyes. Holiness is seen in the eyes. God is seen in the eyes. You can get a real sense of the divine through the eyes of loving people who are close to God.

This concept of the eyes being the window to the soul has its basis in the New Testament, Mt 6:22-23 and in a quote attributed to Cicero, over 100 years prior.

Bryan Foster

Roman philosopher Cicero (1st century BCE) highlights how the eyes interpret the mind's happening. (Oxford Reference)

Matthew is more specific than Cicero. He highlights that both goodness, light, and evil, darkness, will be seen through the eyes. Therefore, the eyes are the 'lamp' to the soul.

"The eye is the lamp of the body. So, if your eye is healthy, your whole body will be full of light; but if your eye is unhealthy, your whole body will be full of darkness. If then the light in you is darkness, how great is the darkness!" (Mt 6:22-23, NRSV)

Conversely, as seen through both the evangelists who wrote Matthew and the philosopher Cicero, our true selves, when evil/dark and lacking in love, will also be seen through our eyes, when we have chosen to move away from God through our beliefs and actions, we move into the darkness, to the evil.

Our eyes tell this story, especially for those aware and who have a well-developed intuitive sense. You may even get a sense from someone who can't look a good person in the eye. There seems to be this natural turning away from the light/goodness/ GODness!

It is as if the 'sun' is too bright for the evil/dark ones. That darkness is where the comfort lies for these people. To come out into the light becomes a real struggle for them.

This is precisely what God wants from and for us all - to come into the light.

To see the error of our ways.

To seek forgiveness and become one with all other authentic, loving people, people of God.

Our eyes are genuinely the windows to our soul. To our authentic, genuine selves.

The Solution is Love

Love will heal our personal and worldly problems. But this needs to be true love seen for what it is, and the source of this love is God. God needs to be turned to for guidance, support, and strength. Only a God-assisted revolution of love will be successful! Humans do not have the capacity or will to do this independently!

The longer-lasting successes throughout history have had God as their supporter. Evil has had limited control, but a loving God defeated these inspired and supported reactions. Or loving action in preparation for, or anticipation of, an evil event.

A misunderstanding of God's place in the world leads not only to ignorance of God but of what our role is, as well.

God is absolute Love. God gives us total Free Will. We decide so much for ourselves. Our personal and communal actions affect so much of what happens in this world. Yes, this cannot explain everything God does or allows to happen. There is an aspect of faith and mystery.

As humans, we cannot expect to appreciate and understand God much at all. God is divine; we are human – a significant distinction and differentiation. It is not until we reach perfection with God in Heaven will we truly know God. However, we can learn so much about God from religious history, history, religious teachings, nature, prayer, etc.

With all this complexity, God is with us and wants the best for all of us. We must work with God towards the equality of all. Those who disagree with equality disagree with God.

Forgiveness

Forgiveness is a most challenging process but an essential need of all humans.

People need to forgive others for their wrongdoing towards them. Others need to forgive us for our failings. We need to forgive ourselves. Forgiveness offered and received is essential for the relationship to repair.

Of course, this is not a simple procedure or one with an inevitable outcome. It depends on so much. It depends on our openness to forgive and to be forgiven. It depends on the person we hurt or who hurt us, being open to forgive or being able to accept forgiveness. It sometimes depends on our ability to offer restitution knowingly or unknowingly to the recipient. It depends on our experience of forgiveness and how we have been affected previously. It depends on our personality, mental, physical, and social health, on our standing with the person concerned, and on so much more.

Once we can forgive and be forgiven and affect restitution as best we can, if necessary, we are set free of sin. We can live more peaceful, fulfilling lives. Our relationships are more robust, and we are happier within these. We are more complete as people living in our families, workplaces, communities, etc.

We must also appreciate and accept God into our earthly relationships. We need to invite God into our relationships to help strengthen these and be there when difficulties arise. When this happens, God is there to support us and help us work through the challenges until the final loving outcome is achieved.

Primarily, out of Love, we are required to place God as the number one in our lives and our relationships. When we can accept this and turn our relationships over to God, we are open to receiving so much assistance willingly and accept the outcomes as part of God's plan.

This is very freeing and something towards which we need to work.

Apologising to God for our hurt caused and the wrongdoings done adds another dimension to our improvement and relationship with God. God always wants the best for and of each of us. God knows intrinsically that we will weaken and make mistakes, hurting ourselves and others along the way. We can't hurt God, but we can freely move away from God through our thoughts and actions. Acknowledging these wrongs and hurts, helps the healing process and brings us closer to our relationship with God. It is God's desire for us.

God loves each of us so much that God needs us all to be as close as possible to each other and God - in true love.

Once we can genuinely forgive and be forgiven…

we are set free.

We are able to live more peaceful, fulfilling, Loving lives.

Moonbeam Capture

A metaphor for our uniqueness, unity, and closeness with Love.

Wherever you are, you cannot escape the capture of the moonbeam.

As you look towards the moon on a clear night, you become the centre of its gleaming light. You are the one literally in the centre! No one in this world is at the centre of the light shining on you! You are exceptional!

An excellent metaphor of Love signalling you out! You are the special one! You are the complete focus of Love's attention - you are it!

Everyone is exceptional with Love. The moonlight shows this more than anything else. Wherever you move, no matter the speed, no matter the time, you are always at the centre! You cannot escape this centeredness. No matter how hard you try, you are always at the centre of the moonbeam - the centre of Love's attention! Equal to all others.

This is an extraordinary invitation to realise the reality of Love and the place you play in this loving relationship.

Another reality could be experienced when under the influence of a direct ray of sunlight. This awesome sunbeam, with all its power and heat and intensity, says much to us about Love and Love's place with each person.

God loves us so much that God wants us to respond to the loving-kindness, compassion, and forgiveness being divinely offered to each of us.

If we can find Love metaphorically in the warmth and the power of the sun, or the gentle peacefulness and quiet of the moon-bean, we are open to experiencing the real God in our lives!

Love calls us to be in a unique oneness with 'Him'! Calling us to be unique yet an integral part of all humankind and calling us to be totally human within His loving embrace!

The moonbeam and sunbeam are just two of Love's many signs used as invitations to us. Love is found in nature and those extra special natural events and happenings. Those 'Wow' moments! Those moments when we just must challenge ourselves to respond to such invitations with a loud, "Yes!"

The moonbeam and the silence of the light gleaming over the sea towards us, as we sit quietly on the seashore, is a holy, Godly experience. We need to be open to experiencing Love in the silence, quietness, and gentleness of the moonbeam.

Love is calling us to be in a unique oneness with each other!

Calling us to be special, yet an integral part of all humankind and

calling us to be totally human within

God's Loving embrace!

Music and Song - Fantastic Inspiration for True Love

Leonard Cohen, Leo Downey, and Elvis Presley – Musicians for God

Karen and I often reflect on three unique and brilliant musicians who have had an incredible impact on our lives and many other people worldwide.

The talents of the following gentlemen go well beyond music and into the Godly realms. They are each very accomplished musicians.

Leonard Cohen (deceased) and Leo Downey Jnr are both now from Canada, while Elvis Presley (deceased) is from the USA. After years as a rock band member, lead singer, and guitarist, Leo moved from California to Canada. These are our most preferred musicians today. Their spirituality and beliefs shown in their music and songs are most often for God, with their unique musical style. Their musical talent is only surpassed by their commitment to God and Love and their willingness to share their beliefs, thoughts, and feelings about many things spiritual and religious. Their music styles so inspire the listener.

Their contemporary music affects us on several levels. Mainly on the loving relationship with God and fellow people level, an integral aspect of each man's music and songs.

Leonard Cohen began the impact on us around ten years ago. My last 'Night of Excellence' introductory prayer segment at Aquinas College in 2009, as the College's APRE, had Leonard's 'Hallelujah' as its main song and theme.

Following is a careful analysis of Leo Downey's unique music and highlights his writing skills in his most reflective book, *Soultracker – Following Beauty.*

Leo Downey

We discovered Leo Downey's incredible musical talents and deep Marian spirituality four years ago when visiting Canada. Staying at Leo's buffalo ranch in spectacular Golden in the Rocky Mountains was marvellous. What brilliant scenery, fauna, and flora! This world is incredibly inspirational. Leo's log cabin is also available for short term leasing

Music and songs written and performed by those close to God have a remarkable impact on so many people searching for God.

Leo Downey is many things, primarily the spiritual, with a considerable commitment to God. His spirituality and religious beliefs are seen in several of his brilliant songs and a book. Leo is truly one of Canada's best-kept secrets. His incredible voice and guitar playing, combined with exceptional lyrics in his songs and passages in his book, call out for others to explore his talent and closeness with God. I have found God in many of his songs, as well. (See Leo's website for Bio, music, and literary details - and so much more.)

Leo Downey, presently from Golden BC in the Canadian Rockies and formerly from California, USA, is an incredibly talented and spiritual man. Leo also runs his buffalo (bison) ranch, linked to his Air B&B log cabin on his most spectacular property surrounded by some of the most outstanding Rockies' scenery imaginable. He shares this property with paddocks of bison/buffalo. And not only these musical and lifestyle choices but also a most accomplished author having written *Soultracker – Following Beauty* with his follow-up book *Soultracker – Following Beauty II* out shortly. http://leodowney.com/about-leo/

Having been fortunate enough to have met Leo while staying in his cabin with Karen, my wife, and our son and daughter-in-law was one of life's most inspirational moments for me. I am also so glad I purchased his self-titled CD, *Leo Downey*. http://leodowney.com/discography/leo-downey-2008/. All his publications and reviews can be found on his webpage.

Leo intermingles his spiritual/religious songs with his everyday rock songs. The lyrics and music of these unique songs are gripping and inspirational. One classic song of Leo's is his *The Tears of Mary* with the words by Leo and Karen Hansen Downey. Interestingly, we found quite a few mini statues of Mary throughout the cabin during our stay.

The Tears of Mary

Words by Leo Downey and Karen Hansen Downey, music by Leo Downey 1995

Pregnant with the future, pregnant with the past
Pregnant with the promised Child, that will take us home at last
Her heart becomes a meadow, her soul becomes a sea
Her Child is her creator, I believe the Mystery
The tears of Mary, are falling in God's eyes
Heaven kneels with a Mother and Child

The truth can be so simple, so innocent and holy
Laying in his mother's arms, a King in all his glory
The tears of Mary, are falling in God's eyes
Heaven kneels with a Mother and Child
You and I were born in the manger
Wise men came with a star
All this time, we have lived to remember
Just how holy we are
The tears of Mary, are falling in God's eyes
Heaven kneels with a Mother and Child

Leo has this beautiful approach with his songs. The spiritual/religious songs do not sound like standard religious songs but are very contemporary, even though recorded a decade or so ago. His strong, talented giving voice and music are exemplified in *The Rest of My Life* being one such song. The most powerful lyrics end the song. There is a solid reference to Mary's virgin birth, as in *The Tears of Mary* song above.

The Rest of my Life (Extract) by Leo Downey

Out of the west, a Pacific swell
Waves of grace curled and fell
The people were blessed, with the soul/song of the Earth
They started again, with a virgin birth

God's Little One by Leo Downey

God's Little One tells a beautiful narrative about a newborn son's first year on earth. The poetic lyrics lift this song to another level once again. His unique style shows Leo's talent in story-telling some beautiful life lessons and experiences in an authentic, spiritualistic, God-loving way.

Leo's Next Album is Coming

Leo is currently working on his next album, which is going back to his music roots, a rock album. His music style is so unique that I can hardly wait for this next record. His strong and appealing God and Mary themed songs will help link his audience to his original rock styles and songs.

God's Little One

God gave us a home where the buffalo roam
Where the blueberries grow and so can our son
The first time I saw him all wrinkled and red
From a pool in the desert, mom and I said
Your first time around the sun
The Lord helped us raise you
Your first time around the sun
My little, our little, God's little One
You were raised in a time, when the world needs a sign
And her love has blown cold, but I'll warm you with mine
REP
Go run with the birds and the bees
Wherever they lead you

Wherever the buffalo roam
They will lead you, they will lead you,
They will lead you home
SOLO
REP

Elvis Presley

Having been around a little after Elvis was claimed as king of rock and roll in the 20th century, it has been a tremendous pleasure listening to and watching as he performs many of his Gospel songs. (See YouTube) With that most incredible voice range singing some exceptionally religious songs, sounding more like rock and roll, though, helps attract people to him and his message – and hence to God.

1. Why me, Lord? 2. How Great Thou Art 3. Take My Hand. Precious Lord 4. Amazing Grace 5. In My Father's House

Must listen to songs include the following three from each very accomplished performer and mystic:

Leonard Cohen's: *'Anthem', 'Hallelujah' and 'Come Healing'.*

Leo Downey's: *'Tears of Mary', 'God's Little One' and 'The Rest of My Life''.*

Elvis Presley's examples: *'Why me Lord?', 'How Great Thou Art', 'Take My Hand. Precious Lord'.*

Two video songs definitely worth watching are: Leonard's *'Hallelujah'*
at https://www.youtube.com/watch?v=YrLk4vdY28Q

And Leo Downey's *'The Rest of My Life'* – particularly check out his spirituality, the scenery, and buffalos/bison... at https://www.youtube.com/watch?v=dS-OblC7c9M

Most of the catalogues of Elvis' Gospel songs have fascinating and entertaining yet powerfully spiritual/religious videos.

We also include the *Rocky Mountain Buffalo Ranch* video we made - for the scenery and feel of the Golden area in the Rockies of Canada. Leo and his buffalos, cabins and majestic backdrops + waterfalls, wolves, and a grizzly bear feature at https://www.youtube.com/watch?v=UCdA2UN5KqA

All Songs from Leo Downey are printed with permission from Leo Downey, including -

http://leodowney.com/discography/leo-downey-2008/http://leodowney.com/about-leo/

Bryan Foster

Social Justice Principles and Human Rights

Social justice principles, inherent in Christianity for two thousand years, are also being taught as 'human rights' by a secular world that 'believes' they invented these principles. However, this is quite important for the secular world. If these principles had remained only as Church teachings, their importance would not reach or affect most of the world's population. The continual present-day denial of so much of the traditional world order, based on the religious principles as taught to us, shows that today's Western world learned little from history and religious traditions and, by its actions or inactions, will possibly take itself into the abyss.

The intellectuals and 'middle to upper' classes have no right to demean those less fortunate. These privileged groups are often repositioning the moral values of others inconsiderately. The wealthy and educated have no right to force their moral values onto the poor. Respect for the values of the poor is critical.

Often, the wealthy's belief that the poor are in control of their lives is misguided and often very wrong. The less fortunate's problems can rarely be solved with the wealthy's unfair solutions. Living in harsh conditions, with little income or reserves, minimal educational and career opportunities, and few or any 'contacts', needs a unique appreciation to attain improvement. Helping the poor to solve their problems would be more successful. This would require the non-poor to be open to the messages of the poor.

Love is the Meaning of Life (2nd ed)

Social justice has been so-called and operative within the Christian religions, especially in Catholicism, since the early 20th century

where it became a significant part of the Catholic teachings. These principles are at the heart and centre of Christianity. And help form the basis of all the social justice teachings of Jesus, Moses, Mahammad, and other religious leaders through the past 5000 years.

Human Rights began after World War 2 in the secular world. The United Nations adopted these in 1948. This Universal Declaration of Human Rights states the freedoms and rights of every person throughout the world. Placing these side-by-side with the social justice principles shows the enormous similarity of both sets. The UN showed how accurate these principles are for all people of all cultures, genuine religions, countries, etc.

Catholic Social Teaching for Best Practice
https://www.caritas.org.au/learn/schools/just-visiting/cst-for-best-practice

The Origins of Social Justice…
https://isi.org/intercollegiate-review/the-origins-of-social-justice-taparelli-dazeglio/

What are human rights
https://www.humanrights.gov.au/about/what-are-human-rights

Bryan Foster

Secularism May Be Dangerous and Possibly Leading Humanity to a Catastrophe!

And now, for what could be a significant challenge for many readers, I would like to ask you to consider something which probably sounds like a threat – which it is not – or something taking away your Free Will and personal beliefs – which it is not also! Please consider what follows as a genuine challenge needing thoughtful consideration before decision making. Your personal belief and considered actions and thoughts for the near future may need time to develop.

Secularism can be considered dangerous and hollow if it lacks substantial depth and belief foundations. It is based on not needing the spiritual world, the world of God, and God! It believes humanity is the only strength and power required for a thriving world. That all answers lie within the human spirit and entity.

How close or distant from the truth could this be? This is where believers and non-believers of God, or secular believers come to an intersection. Authentic people, who aren't fixed in their beliefs, and who are open to many ideas and practices, would genuinely want to explore the arguments for and against secular beliefs and religious beliefs.

In all honesty, who hasn't experienced God in nature, in goodness (Godness), in prayer or meditation, in other people through what they have said or done, which has had a significant impact on them, etc.? Some of these experiences may not show God intrinsically, yet when a person is open to these experiences, God could become 'seen' – felt? Experienced? Tears from God? Feel the Love? Etc.

Many people will have direct experiences with God, where they know in their heart of hearts that God has just made direct contact, e.g., this may happen through any of the experiences listed above. However, God does give various people direct knowledge of God's presence, with the proof being through 'Tears from God'. Tears confirm some message from God. Tears flow, not sobbing as in normal crying, and the believers genuinely feel God's actual presence.

How is secularism leading humanity to a catastrophe?

Firstly, the valued, historical, worldly institutions start to crumble. Respect is lost. The individual becomes the centre of the universe. Broad, accepting communities unravel. Nationalism, communism, narcissism, nihilism, totalitarianism, and many other 'isms' flourish. Already our communities are crumbling. Look at the racism of much of the population, the police and Afro-American killings in the USA, the growing racism and anti-Church/God growth in Australia and Europe, the major racial problems in China, etc.

The lack of respect or even contempt shown to our politicians and journalists. The growing lack of respect for the law, police and legal system. The blaze or even hate-filled reaction to the Church, Islam and other anti-religious/God sentiments growing today.

A massive change in direction for the Western world, along with the attitude of its populations, is needed very quickly. The world as we know it is dying.

Our civilisation is now destroying itself. It is wasting our earthly resources like nothing before. It is destroying people and communities like never. It is very much on its way out! No longer are other individuals and communities fully valued or even respected. The 'Me' world rules. The 'whatever I believe, and think is correct' dominates. The cancel culture is picking up terrible speed! Even though entirely accepted by the great majority of the people, various long-term rights and freedoms are being challenged so much now! 'I am but an island, and there is nothing else of importance – anywhere' - echoes from pillar to screen.

There appears to be little place for higher-order values. A little place for genuinely unique, loving, forgiving people. A little place for God, mostly. This is a guaranteed recipe for disaster.

The onus of contemporary proof of everything has taken the world to the brink.

That everything must be proved by Science is outrightly rejected. Science can only prove or disprove within the physical world. Science does not prove or disprove that those higher forces exist. Science cannot prove or disprove God. God is not physical; therefore, there is no such thing as proving or disproving God with Science.

We need to call out those intellectual elites, atheists and secular fundamentalists who see nothing but the here and now as being accurate. That nothing is everlasting.

Freedom of speech is dying. The overly politically correct subjugate what it is to be truly human - with all humanity's warts and all.

Idealism should be aimed for, but realistically. Following the various religious scriptures with a contextualist approach will help guide us. (That is, Scripture appreciated in the context of the era, culture, beliefs, laws, etc.) A literalistic interpretation of these scriptural sources often leads to misunderstandings and even more problems. Literalists take the scriptural word literally, word for word, with little or no contextual appreciation. Domestic violence in any of its forms at any level of society is never acceptable. Yet, this form of violence is tearing families and relationships apart in all sections of society.

The right to stand up for the real and only loving God is being destroyed by the growing number of atheists and agnostics, who portray themselves as some form of intellectual elites and holders of all truth. Often these groups force their views on others, who they espouse must be ignorant to believe in God. Sure. Don't believe in God if that is your personal belief. But don't try and force or threaten others who believe differently to you.

Many can't forget the most significant examples of atheism in action before it became 'cool' in the 2000s. It was the communist/Marxist Soviet Union; China's communists' massive number of deaths of their populations, be these Chinese or other cultures within their borders. Along with Pol Pot's Cambodia – where millions were killed, executed, and had their lives destroyed in various ways. To name but a few countries and regimes.

Religion was axed as much as these countries could do. No/minimal open worship and following God allowed - yet so much inequality existed amongst murderous regimes - ruling without freedom of choice for the population. Primarily through fear and persecution, after the criminal torturing and mass murders.

Everyone has the right to believe whatever they like, as long as it doesn't hurt others physically, emotionally, psychologically, etc. However, they must search for the TRUTH and not just accept the untruth because they think it to be accurate based on little more than a 'gut' feeling philosophy or something they read, heard, etc.

There are ABSOLUTE TRUTHS. The physical world does exist. Humanity does exist within the physical world. God does exist within the physical and spiritual worlds. We can experience God in so many ways. There is, in general, solid worldly support and need for God! We need what God offers all humanity equally. We need to accept God's absolute love of and for each one of us! Various religious institutions are not supported or even believed in by many of these secularists. Yet, many still believe in a god or superior 'godly' force, somehow related to this world.

Denying God because:

**of the evil actions of others,
or because life isn't fair,
or because we can't understand suffering,
or because we can't scientifically prove God,
or because we believe we don't need God,
or because we see ourselves as so strong that it
would be weak to need God, etc.**

**diminishes our humanity and ability to go
beyond ourselves.**

If religions within our society die, our loving society dies!

The answer to a loving society is found in God's teachings through various genuine religions, prayer, religious experiences, Revelations, and Inspired Messages, etc.

Listen to God's messages in whatever form sent to you,

sent to God's people,

along with your individual experiences of God.

God is the answer – not the problem!

Heretic

One of the best religious books of the past few years is former Muslim, Ayaan Hirst Ali's, 2015, *Heretic: Why Islam Needs A Reformation Now*, Fourth Estate (Harper Collins), N.Y. It is a watershed presentation of understanding, appreciating, and acting against the aggressive Islamic fundamentalists.

Ali's book on the heresies of her former faith, Islam, explains how the west is misinterpreting the real purpose of the violence. According to her lived experience, the Islamic fundamentalists say what they mean. Many Westerners claim it is about poverty or disadvantage, as some have their financial well-being seriously challenged at times. But Ayaan, with all her Islamic experience growing up in a couple of Islamic countries, says that she believes from her direct experience that they honestly claim that they are defending against those anti-Allah, anti-Islam people being the truth. Many attackers are not poor or disadvantaged, she states. They are genuinely in jihad for GOD!

Ayaan's resume is quite spectacular; it includes escaping with her family from her ancestral home in Somalia; her family's escape from Saudi Arabia after seeking refuge there; being a member of the Netherlands parliament, a European parliament, and the recipient of various awards and academic positions at Harvard University, U.S.A.

Unfortunately, because of her publications, presentations, and rejection of Islam, she is on a never-ending 'run'. Leaving Islam made her an apostate needing to continually escape from her 'home' to another 'home' regularly.

One would think that her beliefs have made her life unenjoyable.

This highly principled Arabic lady, who came from a country in extreme poverty, moved across the world, first escaping to Arab countries with her family, then in Europe gaining a parliamentary seat in the Netherlands, and then on to the most extensive and generally considered most powerful and wealthy USA. Here she is protected (to a degree) from the violence chasing her. Her experience, principles and extreme courage are an example for all. She initially received an honorary doctorate but didn't, as it was cancelled due to various Islamic influences in the USA. She did, however, receive some accolades and awards from Harvard University, where she worked.

GOD Loves Aayan.

GOD Loves you.

GOD Loves you both EQUALLY.

GOD Loves ALL equally, All the TIME.

Ayaan Hirst Ali's, 2015, *Heretic: Why Islam Needs A Reformation Now*, Fourth Estate (Harper Collins), N.Y

Inspired Messages for a Loving Life

Why these Inspired Messages (IM)?

The following IMs are more from the everyday philosophy of life.

For the author, these developed over a decade.

Each is aimed at those seeking a more detailed everyday offering of IMs from what has come before in this *Series* since Book 1 in 2016 and Book 7 in 2021.

It also assists those reading this book as their first, or other earlier book, within the *Series*.

Highlighted Inspired Messages to Author Over 10+ years

0 – Scientists mostly agree that the world was created through the Big Bang. Out of pure love, the universe continues to evolve.

1 – Love is pure and absolute. We were all created - you and everyone else, by the total force of LOVE.

2 – Little boys will be boys, and little girls will be girls. They are not little adults. Respect each child as you would adults.

3 – Fire is dangerous. Treat it with respect. Enjoy its beauty and warmth. Put it out before it burns the house down.

4 – Love your mum and dad. Be good. Be polite. It helps make everyone happy, especially you.

5 – School is good. Knowledge is power. Work hard. Achieve. Enjoy your schoolmates.

Take calculated risks within reason. Necessary for growth.

(The nanny state does not help anyone. We must fix litigation laws and allow for various risky ventures.)

6 – Be fair. Stand up for your rights with respect and do not hurt others. Respect your teachers.

7- Change is good. Moving houses for new cultures, environments, people are special + is a bonus.

8 – Justice rules. Do not punish children unfairly. Care for your teeth. Smile.

9 – Make good friends. Keep and value some of them for life.

10 – Sport rules at this age. Develops character and critical physical skills. Boys need significant male influence. Girls need significant female influence. Winning feels good.

(Laugh at the principal's jokes – you never know where this will get you.???)

11 – Develop your gifts and talents to high levels. Try heaps of sporting, artistic and cultural activities to find unique interests.

12 – Welcome adolescence. Allow the changes to happen. Do not fight these. Enjoy your newfound self.

Do not take inappropriate selfies. These will probably bite you at some stage later. Have good friends and stay close to mum and dad for support.

13 – Girls are people first – girls second. Respect them.

Get outdoors often. Play sports and active games.

14 – Limit the payouts. Learn to accept these for what they are. Payouts toughen you up but also cause hurt. Some may get bitchy for a reason based on personal competition. Understand why and help them, and you learn from this.

15 – Technology is good. Learn to use it properly, efficiently and for good reasons. Playtime is good. Please do not listen to older people who may want to use you as a piece of entertainment for their inadequacies. Be careful what you do through the digital age. Once it is out there, you lose control of it.

16 – Porn is terrible. It tries to draw you in. You will become the loser. Your respect for people and you will diminish. Be careful.

17 – Sex/making love is good. Best when in a committed relationship. Respect is essential. Respect yourself and others inherently. No means NO – anything leading to rape or other sexual abuse is not on. Do not play games when you mean NO! Or when you do not mean No.

18 – Life really begins at 18 in the western world. Independence is fun, but the responsibility is critical. Study hard at university, TAFE or in the workplace.

Remember, knowledge is power. It is also often linked to success, money, prestige, and self-worth.

Select a vocation more than a career. Have a passion for your choice. Making some careers all your life could be harmful to your good health. Place yourself in a situation, e.g., necessary qualifications needed to choose your job. Do not choose a boring one, if this is possible. You will regret your choices if these are not in your best selections.

19 – When you find your soulmate, you will know. Do not rush it. But do not let them go just because of your age, your lack of career, your financial situation, etc. You may regret it later.

20 – Do not rush marriage or your desired permanent relationship. It takes time to know if this person is the one for you. People can fake it for you to want them - for some time, even for a couple of years or so.

21 – Value life wholeheartedly. It can be taken at any time. Living is exceptional. We live on a 'knife's edge'.

22 – Live your passion - vocation/career. This should happen if you make the right study/career choices.

Enjoy going to work. Respect your boss and colleagues. Work hard. Aim to achieve and be successful. Extremely rewarding.

23 – Hedonism lacks true humanity. Selfish, greedy people are not pleasant. Keep away from them as much as possible – be aware of their influences.

24 – Have children, if you can and when you are ready. Indeed a most rewarding and life-changing moment. I've noticed that for men, you begin to appreciate others, especially your truth. Adoption may be an option for some – may include international possibilities due to a small number of babies put up for adoption these days. (Abortion has killed the adoption option for many.)

25 – Country towns are community-based. Get into the community. Should experience this lifestyle at some point – preferably early on.

27 – Develop leadership on a professional level. Aim for this aspect if talented and interested. Take opportunities. Early on, be prepared to leave the comfort zone and travel to less 'dynamic' places and in less dynamic vocations.

28 – Family comes first. As your family grows, so does your responsibility and enjoyment within this unit.

29 – Balance lifestyle. Needs to incorporate reasonably: family, career, personal needs, and necessary commitments.

30 – At 30 - Now entirely accepted as an adult within the adult world. No more excuses!

31 – Teamwork is mighty. Life teams. Work teams. Family teams. So much more can be accomplished - a significant extension on the sporting teams, cultural and artistic groups of your youth.

32 – Travel. Overseas travel experiences enhance your appreciation and help develop broader skills needed within the global community. Domestic travel is also magic.

33 – Postgraduate study opens advanced opportunities, both professionally and personally.

34 – Network professionally. Not just for career advancement, etc., but to broaden your sphere of experience and opportunities. Legitimate friendship levels are needed in most cases to depth your personal growth.

35 – Keep in touch with those you value the most. Friendships and contacts will come and go.

36 – Keep fit and healthy. Eat and drink wisely, exercise daily, allow for daily R and R, sleep well (a regular pattern of preparation, bed type, pillow), reflect, evaluate the day.

37 – Pray regularly. Please keep it simple at the start while you get used to this extraordinary time with the all-powerful. For the doubters, if there is an all-powerful massive force and you ignore it, there is still an all-powerful tremendous force with whom you need to relate. If nothing else, this is an excellent form of de-stressing and re-energising. Be careful not to dismiss a solid challenge to acknowledge the Creator and move forward with the all-powerful's Love and help. This could be your moment in time for an incredible advancement ahead – with The Force.

38 - Holiday. Get away from the pressures of life a few times each year, if only for a few days at a time. Do not take work with you. Do not allow work commitments to impose on you unless this is an absolute necessity. Have at least one extended break a year – NO EXCUSES.

39 – Take promotions if of interest. Test yourself. Achieve in higher and/ or different spheres professionally.

40 – Extra-special number 40. Now you should be genuinely feeling and believing who you are. Purity and growth are attained through various activities related to the number 40 for multiple religions. (Principle based on the notion of this day of

40 being extraordinary – for example, aiming for purity and perfection while living your everyday life.)

41 - Adjust your life to incorporate what may be missing or minimal and be prepared to drop or change other areas of weakness that impede you from being you.

42 – The meaning of life is 42 for Monty Pythonesque. (Mine is at 50.) Humour is essential for a healthy fulsome lifestyle, even from Monty Python.

Especially be able to laugh at yourself and with others.

43 - Invest responsibly. Be aware that the most significant risk for high gains is the greatest risk for high losses. Learn how the stock market, investment property, superannuation, and other areas of investment work. Balance your investment risks with your financial stage of life.

43 – Gambling is not good. Only gamble what you can afford to lose. (Quote: from my dad)

44 – Forgiveness is a primary characteristic of love. One of the most challenging necessities. Have the courage to forgive others. Do not forget to forgive yourself as well, when ready and appropriate.

45 – Live a wholesome, humble, and exemplary life as much as possible. Be an excellent living example for your children.

46 – Do something special for someone else every day – but don't tell them. Mix it up along with the beneficiaries. It will help someone have a better day. It will also revitalise your unique place in the universe. The 'butterfly effect' will benefit so many others as well.

47 – Love your spouse in more mature ways as you grow. Allow your relationship to deepen continually. Be proactive.

48 - Be outstanding fathers and mothers, grandfathers and grandmothers to your children and their children. Love them fully. Be solid but fair with your children's upbringing. Be a little less tough on the grandchildren. Being reasonably tough but very fair is their parent's obligation.

49 – Be generous with the unfortunate. Time, money, and prayer are always needed. Take up at least one cause or organisation and give what you can generously.

50 – LOVE is the meaning of life.

51 – God is absolute love. God loves absolutely. God gives us free will to love authentically. God gives us dominion over creation. Out of love, we must respect all of creation, especially each one of us.

52 – Religions' message is simple. It is universal. Love God above all else. Love each other as God loves us. Our decisions must be based on our appreciation of God's commands, our understanding of science and the impacts our choices will have.

53 – G-- the all-powerful does not create wars, violence, starvation, etc. Humanity does it through individual and collective decisions. If G-- is absolute love, then G-- gives us total freedom. Unfortunately, the haves often keep and do not share with the have-nots. Greed rules. The haves have brilliant explanations for their deliberate inactions or actions which harm others. No matter how hard they try to justify such behaviour – their harming is wrong!

54 – Natural disasters are not punishments from G--. Once again, out of love, G-- created the universe and all the principles applied to it. From that time on, it evolved, and the actions occurred naturally.

55 – Pain and suffering are a natural part of life. No one desires this, but we all know of its truth. Pain and suffering often lead to better outcomes when we accept this principle. People are happy to live by the adages: 'no pain no gain' or 'learn from your mistakes or 'you become a better person through adversity, etc. Therefore, relate these to all understandings of pain and suffering.

56 – We can ask why? And why not? Of God the all-powerful. But the bottom line is we do not know. God is divine; we are human. We cannot appreciate God as we are on different levels. We can, however, gain a glimpse of God and God's principles through respecting how Jesus, Mohammad, Buddha etc., lived and taught. Along with the exceptional people throughout history who have lived those principles, e.g., Mother Teresa, Gandhi, Pope Francis, Dali Lama.

57 – Respect all legitimate religions' peoples, beliefs, God, and values. Base the notion of 'legitimate' on the five main world religions of Christianity, Islam, Hinduism, Buddhism and Judaism. Be careful of various sects and cults – judge these on how they relate to the fundamental principles underlying the previous religions listed.

58 – Teachers are angels. They have one of the most, if not the most, necessary professions and yet the most difficult. Their responsibilities are enormous, educating the next generation. More is expected of them virtually every year - Society passes more on to their plate yearly. Society's ills are more and more expected to be solved by teachers and schools. Respect your teachers. Respect your children's teachers. Virtually all have your child's best interests at heart. Do not be critical of them in front of your children. Be mature if there is a challenge and approach them directly. Give them a pat on the back occasionally – remember they often do not see the success of their endeavours. Teachers are ANGELS! Genuinely walk with them. Liberate them with some positive feedback about your child and their student.

59 – Religious leaders, priests, pastors, and teachers, have an essential role within our society. Respect and support them. Their aim is a better, more loving world. A world where all people are treated equally, justly and reverently. A world where God will be seen in every person.

60 – Search for WISDOM. Wise principles come and go in a person's life depending on their circumstances, including their challenges, needs, sorrows, relationships, beliefs, values, self-worth, etc. Hold onto all the wisdom you can. The more fulfilled the lived knowledge each person has, the greater they and all of humanity will be.

61 – There is no authentically 'depthed' Wisdom without God.

62 – Atheists have wisdom from God – they just do not know or believe in its source and requirements! If known by them, then it is a rejection of God – that is exceptionally Evil.

63 - Political correctness has its place, if the basic principles lived by previously are not overrun.

64 - Listen to people with experience. Seek out trustworthy, highly competent advisers, mentors, and information givers. Just because someone says, something doesn't mean they know what they are talking about.

65 - Too often, people will say anything to get your attention/friendship/support, etc. Learn how to weed out the bad from the good. Most people are trying to assist you. Yet, they are sometimes uninformed or lack experience and knowledge of what is needed. Be aware that evil people do exist and keep away physically or figuratively.

66 - No more authentic advice was ever spoken than – If it seems too good to be true, it most often is (in this physical world)!!!

67 - Develop your intuition so that you can initially trust everyone you come across until shown or sensed otherwise. An intuitive response may be quite quick.

68 - Say gidday/hello/how are you, etc., to as many people as possible within the realm of normality who you come across each day.

69 - You are no better a person than anyone else. Your experiences, qualifications, relationships, and successes may imply otherwise – yet you are not a better person. Be humble.

70 - The poor are not in control of their lives – who would choose poverty!

71 - Many rich genuinely misunderstand the poor because they believe that the poor control their lives. This belief gives the rich a free hit. It allows them to ignore the real problems and pretend to assist those less fortunate.

72 - No one got rich through spending. Invest wisely.

73 - Most people do not get wealthy through their career incomes but intelligent investments, including superannuation.

74 - Start saving 10% of income from your first job. Place in a compound interest account or increase your superannuation accordingly, etc.

75 - Compound interest is the secret. You get interest on your interest, as well as on your investment.

76 - Be careful not to over-borrow for investments or lifestyle choices. All borrowings must be repaid in time. Yours and the world's circumstances change. Do not get caught out. Investments are for the long term.

77 - Smart investing in the stock market's shares compared to investment in property virtually equals out over time - different benefits for each. Shares are quick and easy to buy and sell. Houses take time. Some people like to see their investment, e.g. houses – this is a significant appeal for them.

78 - Be aware of significant economic effects which happen regularly. Usually, one major a year. These often are hard to prepare for and are often unseen. Look for the early warning signs, e.g. commercial businesses closing, house prices stagnating or (worse) dropping, shares dropping in value, interest rates falling. Seek professional financial guidance, if necessary. Be prepared to act early.

79 - You may even need to accept financial losses at times not to have more significant losses down the track.

80 - House cycles. Housing values often go through processes – from peaks to troughs and troughs to peak heights. Different cities and towns in the same country usually have differently timed cycles.

81 - Be well prepared for investing. Read. Listen. Converse with the experts. It pays to seek professional advice. Check what their advice is based on whether they have any financial gains because of their advice, e.g. commissions from such investments, which may bias their views.

82 - If possible, get advice from people who have been directly involved with the investment they are purporting. Someone who has achieved financial success now from this investment source should be of a higher value than someone just promoting for their commission or salary.

83 - Each human seems so tiny but is so amazingly awesome. (Look at the person in a rainforest standing within the enormous and multiple trees.) The power and potential to influence world-shattering ideas and creative options within the brain to achieve so much are boundless. A universal paradigm is possible and expected of each individual.

84 – Give your full attention to the person you are communicating with. It shows respect, allows for accuracy and good recall and allows each person to feel valued.

85 – Computer games, social media, the internet, texting, etc., can become addictive and diminish your life. Be careful and seek help if this becomes apparent to you or your friends and colleagues.

86 - Do not hit a person when down. Never stomp or kick on the ground. Both are evil actions. One punch can kill; imagine what the boot could do to a person's head?

87 - Beauty is exceptional. Love it. Be responsible. A beautiful looking person needs to respect all others. You have a gift, most others desire. Responsibly appreciate others own beauty as a person, within themselves, etc.

88 - Age brings wisdom, which is quite exciting. Youth brings energy, drive, speed, enormous hope, plans, etc.

89 - When wisdom and youth are brought together, magic happens. Young be open to the older. Older be available to the younger!

90 - Allow all people to be themselves, no matter how different to you they may be. Exemption – evil ones.

91 - Life truly is short. Allow each moment to be something special to you in the whole scheme of things, no matter how little or large it may be. Treat the mundane, everyday life as wholesome and the backbone/basis for all the exciting and disappointing times that inevitably come.

92 -Develop actual, wholesome, and good values. These will hold you in good stead. Good guys do win. SOMETIMES HARD TO SEE.

93 - Manners are powerful.

94 - Be able to mix with the powerful and the powerless alike. Confidence in yourself and YOUR life's triumphs are the basis for this possibility. Mix with all sorts of people for a well-balanced appreciation of life and gain the ability to lead a life for the betterment of all people with whom you come in contact.

95 - Good value mostly keeps the economy and communities functioning well. Cheap kills off both eventually.

96 - Do what you must do. If it is right and good.

97 - Be a man – not a wimp. Yes, it can get tricky – but look after yourself also. Look after your wife and children thoroughly! Be sensible and do not place them in danger.

98 - Be open to the wonder and awe of our universe.

99 - Know the difference between the sensual and the lustful. The sensuality of this world is fantastic when seen in a beautiful and not grubby way.

100 - These are my 100 pieces of wisdom I believe are essential; number 100 says that I may become wiser with more experience and that I should be open to adjusting these other 99 wisdom statements as I listen to more people, experience more of the world and people, listen to God, etc.

101 - There is never too much wisdom if the wisdom is the Truth.

102 – Communicating face-to-face is the most personable and trustworthy way.

103 – Digital age communication devices are a resource, not an 'appendage'. Each has its place but not to be the sole device.

N.B. Financial Disclaimer –

I, Bryan Foster, the author of these investment quotes, am not a financial adviser or accountant. These pieces of financial advice in this book need to be checked with qualified financial planners, etc., before deciding on your investment pathway.

Seek professional financial guidance from trusted sources and act accordingly. Be prepared to act early. You may even need to accept financial losses at times so as not to have more significant losses down the track.

Conclusion for Book 8A

Love is the Meaning of Life (2021) is an essential book within this *Series* (2016-2022). It highlights another pathway to Life, Love, and existence for humanity. Love is the most crucial life aspect of all. It is what we need for a safer and more rewarding, and loving world. Our beliefs, lifestyles, ethics, morality and the strongest of all relational feelings, Love, is at the centre of us, our families and friends, our working colleagues, and all others attracted to Love. Most of the faithful believe it is out of the divine, creator's destiny that we exist. The aim of Salvation with God in Heaven is the approach needed for believers. Unfortunately, many non-believers who are rejectors of God may never achieve this.

Cosmopolitan lifestyles, which require Love to help make life fair and reasonable for all, are often shared through believers and non-believers alike. Even though the faithful are steadfast in belief in God's place in our universe, they can still accept and respect others, e.g., secularists, as authentic humans on a life journey, maybe to find God or God's ways within our world.

Did humanity come from a world of Love, whole and primarily complete? Or did we evolve as living organisms like all other fauna and flora historically? All lifeforms have souls, the lifeforce. (i.e., God with/in them…) For the author, these beliefs were discerned over decades.

Love is the Meaning of Life. This is the key theme for this eighth book in the *'God Today' Series* (2016-2022). We can discuss life, death, and salvation from the Love perspective, without mentioning God. Secularists happily live and enjoy life: 1) without believing in God, or 2) having God assist them, overall. But is this the best interpretation of our lives' Love Story? Book 6 explains the Love=God story and Love's impact on our world today. Book 8A has been written primarily from the secularist's perspective, but with links, explanations, challenges, etc., from God included. These weren't included to confront or diminish the secularist's view of Love and Life! Just to add another dimension to explore with an open mind and genuine passion to find out about Love.

What do we need for Loving salvation if this exists, and we only require Love on this earth? There would be no necessity for a divine existence ruling, leading, and creating everything? The people of faith believe in the evolving lifeforms in the readiness for the end of the world, the forthcoming Jesus. They may even include Mahommad for Muslims. Both Jesus and *Mahomad are God's Incarnates. (See Book 5, *Jesus and Mahomad are GOD* [Incarnate].) God is becoming fully man/woman, then returning as God in Heaven. Allowing for our varying understandings and appreciations, we hopefully will discover God's love for all creation. God will assist all those close, and others trying to be close, to 'Him'. Saved by our One and Only GOD of all time, for all people forever, for all religions!! (See Book 1, *1God.world: One God for All.*)

It seems quite a while back now that I was experiencing God as a teenager and early '20s relatively young person. This included the yearly private chat at school with a priest from the local archdiocese or other priestly vocations' groups - encouraging vocations to the priesthood. I recall this was over the years 10-12. I also recognised that I enjoyed what the vocations' priests were offering me each year, especially about God in our world and the communal relationships of the priests. However, I chose marriage instead of the priesthood as my special divine calling. Education also called, and I ended up teaching for forty-two years. As an author, I am continuing my post-teaching education vocation of informing various groups worldwide about God, Love and divine relationships with God for us all, etc. And how God works.

The Love of God for 'His' creations of humanity, fauna and flora, the cosmos and all creations which have the souls of life are what helps bring us closer to being with God, Love and Salvation in Heaven. Souls = Life.

(*Mahomad is spelt here in the most used spelling by God when revealing God's 21 Revelations to the author.)

8B

Selections from Book 6

Love is the Meaning of Life: GOD's Love

(1st ed)

Introduction

Why this Section 8B?

The following edited sections from Book 6, *Love is the Meaning of Life: GOD's Love*, are aimed at those seeking more detail or a refresher from what has come before in this *'GOD Today' Series* since Book 1 in 2016 and up to Book 7 in 2021.

It also assists those reading this book 8A, *Love is the Meaning of Life*, as their first, or other earlier book, within the *Series*.

Even though the lengths of a few sections are reasonably long, the included detail is essential for many readers to continue developing the key points within each book of the *Series*.

Hopefully, the reader may become interested in this other book through the articles and sections, which may allow them to explore more about God, Love and the Relationships of Humanity, if they so choose?

CONTENTS 8B

Selections & Author Articles from Book 6

Love is the Meaning of Life: God's Images (1st ed)

Revelations and Inspired Messages (IM) from God

Love is the Meaning of Life (2nd ed)

Other Discerned Truths by the Author from God

Content Summaries for Books 1-7

Bryan Foster

What are the Revelations and Inspired Messages from God?

This *Series* refers to Revelations as those inspired messages from God through a unique encounter with God and the person receiving them. However, there should also be some form of 'proof' of this reality, such as the 'Tears from God' and other justification points (explained shortly) before it is entirely accepted and shared as the Truth. Inspired messages are those thoughts and issues received through prayerful experiences or other people, nature, or events -from wherever God inspires us. However, a discernment process is needed to clarify this authenticity, unlike ordinary thoughts and feelings.

The concept of 'Revelations' in this *Series* is also referred to as 'Special or Direct Revelations' in various religious circles in society and academia. God specifically directs these Revelations to individuals or groups. What is referred to as 'inspired messages' in this publication may, at times, be referred to as 'General Revelations' in other religious publications and discussions? These are from God to anyone in general, being received through such means as nature, ethical appreciations, and cognitive reasoning. (GCSE, BBC) Christianity believes that Jesus is the ultimate example of Revelation's fullness on this earth by humanity. (Oxford Scholarship, 2018) The different religions have various appreciations of the relevance of Revelations historically and today. All genuine religions believe that God reveals Godself to this world through various forms, especially through people, their beliefs and morality, and the natural world.

The terms 'Revelation' and 'inspired messages' are used as points of clarity. Naming every message God inspires humanity with the word 'Revelation' may become confusing as different Revelation levels exist. 'Revelation' is used when there is direct contact of God with specific people, while 'inspired messages' are for those Revelations discerned by people as emanating from God. How both occur is explained.

Series' Books 1, 3, and 5 primarily explain the various Revelations I received directly from God in 1982, 2016, and 2018, along with the inspired messages received from God and discerned over more than thirty-five years. There is an inherent, authentic sense of the Truth being shared.

The literary style states the Revelations and inspired messages received or discerned from God accurately without diminishing the emphasis of each through diplomatic, political, or politically correct forms.

The key Revelations and inspired messages will be stated clearly and without softening to appease certain groups who may not fully or partially agree with each statement. Each Revelation and inspired message will be explained in enough detail to make the point succinctly and clearly.

There is a real emphasis on Keeping it Simple for God's People. It is a positive approach, not a negative one. Too often, religious preachers, teachers, and theologians emphasise too much detail beyond the message's clarity. People then get lost in all the detail, and the point from God is missed. In the *'GOD Today' Series*, these books aim to keep the messages simple yet explained with enough detail to gain a proper understanding.

These books are not apologetic works. It is not teaching or preaching a set of one religion's doctrines over other faiths. It is not standing up and fighting for any religion or religious leader or any specific religion's beliefs or faith patterns.

Each is a Book of the Truth and inspired from the forever One and Only God of existence to the author.

All genuine religions are equal and have an essential role from God for each of their followers. The belief in only one God is most liberating and beneficial for appreciating and following God.

This Truth is the Truth of God for today's global and interconnected world. The following section explains why I make this claim.

It has been quite a journey to get to this point. It began in 1982 when receiving the Tears from God and physical warmth flowing from head to foot received as part of the gift of healing from Sister Ann at a secondary school's Commitment Day where I was teaching. Over the interim period from 1982 until now, so much has been discerned as God's inspired messages. This discernment process is explained, with many inspired messages recorded throughout this *Series*.

After receiving God's Revelation in 2016, explained in various ways and sections throughout this *Series'* of books (1-9), the initial reaction was one of doubt - even though there were many 'Tears from God' (See section 6 'Tears from God' following for details) on many occasions privately and with my wife, Karen, to show its authenticity and genuineness.

When it came to the crunch to decide what would be highlighted in the first book in this *'GOD Today' Series*, *1God.world: One God for All*, I couldn't run with all the Revelations. I only highlighted the 'One God Only – One God' Revelation and some subsequent discerned inspired messages from God and stories of experiencing God throughout my life. A real doubting Thomas scenario occurred. In hindsight, I now believe this was all part of God's plan. God initially wanted me to highlight the One God Only Revelation, along with the messages and stories contained in that edition.

This approach used for the first book in this *'GOD Today' Series* opened the opportunities for me to grow into the other Revelations these past five years and to discern a better appreciation of each. To also gain the courage to go out into the world and state these with authority. It was not just a matter of listing these but believing strongly in each one and explaining each in the detail God wanted to be enacted. God wanted these Revelations to become part of the world's meaningful and fully understood religious and Godly lexicon.

Many people worldwide probably also received these same or similar Revelations and inspired messages over various periods and years. Maybe even identical times and dates as me? How they reacted to this experience and how they took its necessity to be promulgated throughout the world would be quite valuable to know about and to see.

We all need to appreciate these Revelations and Inspired Messages (IM) and what these mean so that we can each make the Revelations and IM an integral part of our lives.

'Revelation' Descriptions as used in this Series?

Revelations appear to the receiver to be 'spoken' by God, through the 'mind's eye', (e.g., usually in the early morning hours for this author).

Inspired Messages are 'felt/experienced' as from God and discerned by the author (e.g., most are eventually written down or seen as reflections and discerned messages by this author).

Vital/Key Points are primarily discerned and experienced, often over long periods, as known to be the Truth from God and significantly add to the details inspired by God. These are the 'everyday sort of information from God to whoever requires God's assistance'.

(Edited Extract from *Where's God? Revelations Today*, 2018, by Bryan Foster, p35-38)

Revelations and Inspired Messages (IM) from GOD to Bryan Foster for Today's World. Most Revelations were revealed in 2016 and 2018. IM are from over the decades of the author's life

GOD gave the author 21 Revelations in May 2016 (15) and November 2018 (6) for today's world. Both Revelations were given to Bryan around 3 am, at two different venues at the base and on the plains of Mt Warning / Wollumbin, Australia.

Referencing in this *Series'* books: Primary source = GOD. Secondary sources = books, websites.

There is ONLY ONE GOD for all people, religions, and cultures-for all time - past, present, and future. (Rev. #10)

Jesus and *Mahomad are both Incarnations of GOD (* Spelling as revealed mainly by GOD to Bryan) (Rev. #15)

GOD IS ABSOLUTE LOVE (Discerned by author in this sense.)

GOD says that we are ALL EQUAL and LOVED EQUALLY by GOD (Rev. #9).

God's Revelations Book 3, # 1-21, Rev #1 to 12 (p.63ff.); Book 5, Rev #15 p.(118ff) Rev #16-21 (p.137ff.); Rev #6 (p.155); #13 (p.161); #14 (p.164f.) -

1. Be Truthful
2. Do not be Greedy
3. Love life – don't take it
4. Respect all
5. Love one another as I have loved you
6. Die for what is right

7. Be educated for what is correct & truthful
8. Education is paramount for all
9. We are one
10. One God only – One God

> "I am a prophet Prophets are true" (This is close to the physical placement and punctuation in the Revelations received, i.e., after number ten and on the right bottom of the page. Is it referring to the author?)

11. God's messages to a world in need
12. This world is in enormous need
13. Cyberbullying – in all its forms, of all sorts, of all ages.
14. Fear rules – often from the cyber world eliminate this
15. God is Jesus & Mahomad
16. We need God
17. We need to be vulnerable to God
18. We need to be asking for God's help continually along with assistance & support – always. 'No ego blowouts' – Just ask for help. Always.
19. We are insignificant compared to God
20. God is so superior – face up to it. Believe it! Stop fighting it!
21. Be meek & humble & real

Revelations #1-15 from 29 May, 2016, received on the plains at the foot of Mt Warning, Murwillumbah Showgrounds, NSW Australia, after being awoken in the early hours of the morning while staying in my caravan/trailer.

Revelations #16-21 were received at Mt Warning Rainforest Park at approx. 3 am on 3 November, 2018.

The following few pages in Book 5 (p.137ff) explain each of the last six Revelations' discerned meaning, i.e., for #16-21.

All Humans, Fauna and Flora are Soul-Filled and Divine at Birth! That is GOD's LOVE for all lifeforms on this Earth. (Discerned by author in this case.)

GOD desires for us all to go to Heaven at death. Yet we have the final choice decided together with GOD about where we will go – Heaven or Hell.

The Secular World needs a Reformation. GOD is highly NEEDED in today's world. (Rev. #11, 12, 16, 17, 18. Book 3 p.209ff)

Islam needs its Reformation – (See Ayaan Hirsi Ali, author of *Heretic: Why Islam Needs a Reformation Now*, 2015.) (Book 3, p.209ff)

Science is GOD's gift to humanity and the world. It is needed to help appreciate God's creations and improve the world. (See Book 3, p. 195ff)

GOD's unique, photographic SIGNS were taken by the author for GOD to encourage people to believe that the Revelations and Inspired Messages, etc., shared by the author are from GOD, to assist them to believe in the Revelations, etc. gifted from GOD to Bryan.

See many unique and quite startling images in Book 4. See image explanations in Book 3 p.148ff. These include sun arrows, sun rays, sun flares, a double rainbow, along with a giant Easter sun cross taken one week after Easter at Texas, southern Qld.

Each day is a gift from GOD. We need to treat it as such. We are called Home to GOD when GOD is ready.

'Tears from God' are gifts from GOD to help people realise GOD's closeness to them and that GOD's Revelations and Inspired Messages are authentic. (See Book 5, p.34, 82ff.) (There are enough examples seen worldwide and written about over the centuries for these to be genuinely real.)

GOD sent Bryan six Inspired Messages on the afternoon before the 15 Revelations were revealed and received on the following night in May 2016. (See Book 3, p113ff)

> GOD has permanent Tears from God [Closeness with lifeforms.]

> GOD is not the warrior image. [But the Absolute Love image.]

> But is the loving, caring, for all others. [Lover]

> Our bodies are indeed the Temple of GOD. [God is fully present with each of us.]

> Purify [our body].

> Don't harm, poison it…illicit drugs, smoking.

GOD seems to have invited the author to be a prophet and espouse GOD's 21 Revelations. (See Book 5 p.20, 88ff) (The author has discerned the legitimacy and reality of this invitation. Tears from God were sent for both Karen and me as proof.)

I will continue presenting any Revelations and Inspired Messages from God - e.g., through being the author of the nine books in the '*GOD Today*' *Series* initially; then, over time, I will add new websites and also add to the present websites, and videos already published.

Are the Revelations and Inspired Messages contained in this Series the Truth from God?

YES – I'll Explain...

Truthful, Genuine and Authentic Explanations

As an author, extolling the Revelations and inspired messages from God is a most challenging task. It goes well beyond my reflective writing of some thoughts and meanings. It goes to the whole core of appreciating ourselves, humanity, and our association with God. To claim the authority was given by God to do so is a massive personal challenge. Rest assured, it hasn't been done lightly. There is considerable truly heartfelt anxiety.

I genuinely believe in everything written in this publication wholeheartedly in my heart of hearts, my soul of my soul, as God gave me.

The collection is one author's Revelations and inspired messages from God. Others throughout the world will also probably be receiving similar Revelations and inspired messages. Some may put these into publications. We all have our ways of dealing with and propagating what we receive.

All people can receive God's messages and Revelations. The big question for each person is, Am I ready and open to receiving messages or Revelations from God? Would I know when I received any? What would I do with these if and when I had similar experiences to this author? God inspires us in many ways, mainly through other people and nature. Am I aware of inspired messages from God through others and our world?

These Revelations and inspired messages revealed to me have developed over at least forty years. It is not something that has just ensued. The culmination has been the 21 Revelations from 2016 to 2018 at Murwillumbah Showgrounds and the Mt Warning Rainforest Park in NSW, Australia.

The critical reasons for believing that these Revelations and inspired messages are from God are more detailed. The specific reasons below are followed by the detail of each subsequently.

- the 25th birthday experience and Revelation of God in May 1982;
- the Tears from God experiences, which have been growing in intensity and frequency, especially in the most recent years;
- the recent spectacular photographic images highlighting metaphorical or direct links with God;
- coincidences and signs from God over many years, especially in these past four years;
- the Revelations from God at the foot of Mt Warning in May 2016 and November 2018;
- the longevity without any personal doubt of my strong association with God;
- the personal career/vocation, 42 years teaching religion from years 1-12, including 30 years of Study of Religion to senior years 11-12;
- holding senior leadership positions in religious schools and parishes;
- prayer and meditation throughout and
- the continued strong support and agreement from my wife, Karen, and our families and friends.

Each of these reasons supports the belief in either the Revelation or inspired messages from God. God never forces anyone to believe anything. There is a level of 'proof' but also the mystery of the faith with any Revelation or inspired message from God. Therefore, through the combinations of these reasons and others, God's unique presence is experienced with the outcomes that need to be shared. Having always been close to God, or at least in my teens on the fringes, allows for that openness to hear and know intrinsically when something is legitimately from God.

The 25th birthday experience is explained in detail. I believe the longevity of living without any doubt about God since that 25th birthday experience is quite significant. Since that 1982 experience, when God came to many students, staff, and me on the schools' 'Commitment Day' is exceptional. The unique connection with God when prayed over by a charismatic religious sister/school principal who also had a master's degree in psychology is outstanding and very rewarding. There has been absolutely no doubt about God's existence or God's absolute equal love for each human person throughout history. This 1982 revelatory moment was when I first truly experienced Tears from God in such depth. As well as the incredible warmth flowing from Sister's hands placed on the top of my head downwards through my whole body.

From that moment almost forty years ago, there have been some tough and challenging times, as there are for everyone over their lifetimes. For me, these were mainly of personal health and financial types. Some were life-threatening or life-changing beyond any expectation or plan. There was also the average life challenging experiences of others. These range from family to global. The global challenges needing to be

Bryan Foster

worked through include war, poverty, and other injustices throughout the world and God's place with all these. Then there are the direct challenges in your beliefs, particularly from atheists. Many members of this group are becoming particularly vicious and hate-filled towards anyone who espouses faith in God. You must wonder why this is their form of defence/attack? There must be something more – do they feel guilty? Insecure? Ignorant? Unloved? Intellectually challenge? I just wish they could be open and deliberately give God a go. We must challenge these people out of love for God and the Truth. Stop hiding from the Truth. The Truth will set you free!!! For me, this hateful reaction was experienced directly when I opened myself up to various religious sites on social media to introduce my first *GOD Today' Series* book, *1God.world: One God for All in 2016.*

The Tears from God's experiences have been growing in intensity and regularity in recent years. These were initially experienced in 'introductory' levels from about fifteen in year ten when I first wondered if I would like to join the priesthood through to a higher level while at teachers' college in my late teenage years. One significant and influential event while at college was visiting a Sunday night Catholic charismatic mass where people were being healed through the Holy Spirit. The 25th birthday moment was the first significant Tears from God moment for me. Since then, similar sorts of occasions have been potent and enhancing. Each shows those extraordinary moments of pure bliss and the presence of God. I receive these tears as a sign of proof for something God gave me, said to me, which I felt, etc. These are different to normal tears, e.g., no sobbing, etc. Tears just run from the eyes, controlled by God, I would imagine.

The 'Tears from God' are the primary means of knowing God's unique presence and occasion of confirming those Revelations or inspired messages.

In 2016 at the foot of Mt Warning, I was awoken and told by God in my mind's eye to write down precisely as God sent me the Revelations. The 3 am early morning encounter with God is in the 'Mt Warning…' story throughout this *Series*. This supernatural Revelation was confirmed the following morning at a First Communion Mass in the nearby church where I married Karen forty-three years ago this year – through a Tears from God moment. Once again, two years later, more Revelations occurred at the foot of Mt Warning. These are those numbered sixteen to twenty-one.

There have been different experiences, often recorded as photographs and featuring the sun, which shows God telling a story or offering a particular message. This message may be metaphorical or literal. Often it is God giving a sign of support or confirmation of that specific message. A point of encouragement to the message's authenticity and the need for it to be shared with others. In my case, the need to accept my place in the scheme of God's plan and to go and do whatever is required to propagate the Revelation or message is also a genuine aspect!

In 2018 there were five quite similar sunlight events to each other, in close time proximity. One occurred at the foot of Mt Warning just after sunrise, another at Texas on the NSW/Queensland border, a third was at Straddie, North Stradbroke Island. Another two occurred at Kingscliff and Cabarita beaches in northern New South Wales, close to Mt Warning, Australia. These images are part of the overall

Bryan Foster

methods God uses to make points. These are just one method of many, though.

Coincidences and signs often point to special moments. In *Where's God? Revelations Today Photobook Companion: GOD Signs (2nd ed)* these are explored along with previously mentioned various sunlight experiences. Many of the images seem so incredible. Some might even wonder if the photos had been enhanced. Not so, though. (One exception, though, is the image of Mt Warning with a small cloud atop its peak. The image needed different colours to give genuine authenticity to that photo's sun's rays emanating from the cloud and travelling outwards and upwards.)

The career/vocation choice to teach and specialise in religion eventuated with forty-two years of teaching religion in religious schools. Needing and strongly desired, starting each school day and religion lesson with God's communication is incredibly empowering. Class prayer and meditation were highly significant for all these years. For thirty of these years, the academic Study of Religion classes for years eleven and twelve required the spiritual dimension and the intellectual dimension. This subject needed an intimate knowledge and considerable experience, if possible, of the various religions of Christianity, Islam, Judaism, Buddhism, Hinduism, and Australian Indigenous Spirituality. Teaching religion on these multiple levels every working day for an extended time develops a genuine spiritual relationship with God for the teacher especially, and to a degree for the students. A truly loving relationship with the Divine hopefully develops over those crucial years of life, getting to know God on a very intimate level! Your day is so much God-based. You truly get to appreciate God from each religion's perspectives and beliefs.

Combine this with your own daily prayerful and meditative relationship with God, and a teacher of religious faith has something exceptional and unique from which to share.

Senior leadership positions in schools and parishes help develop your relationship with God. These positions resulted from the personal, academic background being based on Theology, Scripture, Liturgy, and Religious Education, from experience gained in schools, and personal spirituality being shared. Each qualification up to a master's degree has multiple levels of religion covered. Whether you are leading a school as principal or leading the religious school's religious aspect as an assistant principal, or senior school levels as a Year 11 or 12 Coordinator, you should exemplify and live your relationship with God, your faith, and beliefs. You are challenged daily with everyday human aspects of others' relationship with God, religion, the religious school, etc. Through all this, your relationship with God grows and strengthens.

Senior parish roles result in similar experiences to the religious school but on a parish or deanery level. A deanery is a geographical grouping of various local parishes. It is led by the leadership priest, who is known as a Dean. In my roles of Chair or Secretary of the parish or deanery, pastoral councils place you as a non-clergy leader, primarily for both the service and visionary aspects. You are there to help facilitate your parish or deanery congregations' spiritual, religious, and pastoral growth as a laity help for the priests. Through experiencing the challenges as best of all for these people you deal with through these roles, you cannot help but be strongly influenced by their challenges, successes, and failures in life and their relationships with God and each other. The influence this has on strengthening your relationship with God is substantial.

When you have an authentic, prayerful relationship with God, so much of God's truth becomes apparent for these faithful. The impact is positively life-changing. You so much trust in God. God helps you through good and bad times. You have genuine compassion and empathy for humanity. God is indeed central to your existence.

The commandment about placing God as Number One and Only One, across all genuine religions, becomes accurate and actual. You then naturally aim to love each other as God does. This prayer, meditation, and action with God's sent lifestyle, as exemplified by Jesus and Mahomad (See Book 5), both being God Incarnate. Other 'Incarnates' probably also exist. As their reality becomes known and supported, they will be more open to God and more prepared to discern God's messages for themselves and others. Discernment of God's Words becomes not just natural but an essential part of your life.

Karen, my wife (and 'angel') of forty-three years, is integral to my relationship with God.

Karen adds the depth needed to encounter God in these unique ways.

She helps me understand and appreciate God's messages and Revelations through her unwavering support and openness to discuss each moment, each experience, each Tear from God encounter.

GOD LOVES US ALL EQUALLY

…[there is] the need to accept my place in the scheme of God's plan and to go and do whatever is required to propagate the Revelations or Inspired Messages!

(Are you, the reader, ready?)

If not, you may need to work towards this readiness.

I genuinely believe in everything written in this publication and *'God Today' Series* wholeheartedly,

in my heart of heart, and soul of soul…

All are God's messages and Revelations

(when stated as such)!

Greater detail for these explanations above follows.

Where the Wisdom for the '*GOD Today' Series* all began - Author's 25th Birthday Revelation

The day doubt disappeared, and my faith journey went to an unimagined higher level. I gained a whole new perspective of GOD and GOD's part in my life on this day. Tears from GOD's love were experienced for the first time. The doubt about the reality of GOD disappeared. 'Let Go and Let GOD' became an actual spiritual reality of a profound order.

The stars all seemed to have aligned. It was my 25th birthday in 1982. As well as the school's uniquely offered annual 'Commitment Day'. It was also my last day at this school. At the end of the day, I left this school for my first country school principalship – which began on the Monday after leaving Brisbane.

It started with birthday excitement but the last day of school sadness and ended in tears of absolute joy and oneness with GOD.

This school was unique in its philosophy and enrolment policy. One key difference to most schools was their strong association with the charismatic Catholic movement. This was especially manifested in the annual 'Commitment Day' to GOD. Various staff had unique gifts from GOD, which they actively used within the charismatic movement, but are not limited to this movement. Many people have these multiple gifts from GOD but often aren't aware of such gifts. The other common one is Speaking in Tongues, which I have witnessed on many occasions. On this day, the seven teachers with the charismatic gift of healing were engaged for much of the time, healing students and teachers alike. This healing encompasses any weaknesses, e.g., physical, emotional, or social.

On this day, the students and staff of this junior secondary Brisbane Catholic school began the day with a special Mass celebrated by a charismatic priest from Melbourne. The mass was followed by an invitation to students and staff to commit to GOD sometime throughout the day. There was no compulsion, though. The students could roam the school freely throughout the day, with the only prerequisite being no noise near the church. Staff supervised.

The staff of fourteen had seven charismatic teachers who had the spiritual gift of healing. One of these, the principal, was a sister in a religious order. Many of these charismatic teachers, plus the priest, presented at various positions within the church throughout the day. Students could choose who they would like to pray with when offering their commitment to GOD. Most stations would have many students continue with the staff member.

I sat with a particular student during the mass. This student was in a few of my classes. After mass concluded, it took about an hour for this student to ask me to pray with the principal and her present students. It was quite an event to get their due to various challenging circumstances. However, once there, we were invited by the principal to move to the front of her group of eighteen to twenty students. Sister asked this student if she would like us to pray for her. She then asked me if I'd like to place my hand on the student's shoulder and pray. I agreed and prayed for her from deep within my heart and soul - no speaking in tongues, just everyday English.

This belief in prayer causing healing, however, had caused me significant challenges that morning. I was tearing myself apart inside through the doubt that enveloped me about the whole healing circumstances that had been occurring in the church that past hour. Not being a charismatic person and having significant doubts about the entire healing process through prayer over action caused me significant concerns. Much of this doubt was based on the television evangelists we would see on Sunday morning television back in the 1970s and 1980s, where people were miraculously 'healed' in large numbers before our very eyes as if this was the norm. There was truth to many of these healings, yet there was always so much doubt, as well. It was remembered that many of these tele-evangelists eventually admitted to fraud or other inappropriate behaviours. I witnessed charismatics healing at a local Brisbane parish while eighteen years of age and at teachers' college. This had impressed me enough to want to consider it more. The tele-evangelists over the previous years until this Commitment Day made belief in this healing process exceedingly tricky.

So, as I walked this young lady to Sister, I was in incredible anguish internally. I was fighting against the possibility of something extraordinary. Each group had crying or sniffling people, and all were arm in arm with each other. It seemed to be too much for this doubter. Once Sister asked me to pray for the young lady, I instantly decided to 'Let Go and Let GOD'. This freeing moment was something quite unbelievable. The confusion and doubt turned to belief and love. Sister then placed her hands on the girl's head and prayed. At that moment, the student broke down, and tears freely flowed. I was now also tear-filled.

Next, Sister asked if I'd like her to pray over me. What followed was life-changing. As she placed her hands on my head and prayed, there was this incredible feeling of heat flowing from my head downwards to my feet. I broke down and cried tears of absolute love for GOD and those around me. This is the moment in time that all my confusion, doubts, and challenges about GOD disappeared.

Later that afternoon, I asked Sister what had happened, and she explained that GOD came into me and that my old self was 'washed away' (downwards) and that I was 'filled up' with the new me.

I have remained so faith-filled and full of GOD's oneness and awe ever since – that is 36 years. My faith has never wavered since that day, even when some very challenging issues have confronted me. GOD was with me through each of these.

That was the day I truly learned that tears, in specific instances, are a sign from GOD - that GOD is truly present at that moment.

I am often asked if a similar experience of how GOD came to me, along with the Tears from GOD, will happen to others, my students, their families, friends, colleagues, etc. I genuinely believe that it could if the opportunity availed itself. We need to accept GOD's offer, whenever and wherever made. We may need to search out the possibilities. We may not expect it when it does happen. I believe the secret is always to be open to receiving GOD in both expected and unexpected ways. GOD loves us beyond our imagining and wants the best for each of us. We must not be blinded to GOD by all the distractions of this world. We need to be prepared for GOD to come in whatever way GOD chooses. It may not be what we expect, though.

We need to clear our minds and hearts to the beauty, purity, and awesomeness that is GOD. We need stillness, openness, and desire to accept whatever GOD offers, whenever GOD provides it.

The notion in much of the western world today is that we don't need GOD. It is either because we have so much or because we are blinded, which is an absolute fallacy.

We need GOD as much today, if not more than at any time and at any place in history have needed GOD.

It is the first significant time in history that the belief in GOD and acceptance of GOD being with us on this earth is diminishing. It is a time of absolute urgency requiring a major cultural shift towards GOD and GOD's people here today.

…there was this incredible feeling of heat flow from my head downwards to my feet.

I then broke down and cried 'Tears from God' (no sobbing) (see p.260) - of absolute Love for God and those around

This is the moment in time that all my confusion, doubts and challenges about God disappeared – so far forever.

(Edited Extract from *Where's GOD? Revelations Today*, 2018, by Bryan Foster, p131-135)

Mt Warning/Wollumbin – Word of GOD Revelation – the Wisdom Story

In 2016 GOD 'came down' from the mountain. This most majestic Australian 'mountain' in the Northern Rivers, NSW, offered a most remarkable GOD experience for the author. Having just spent three days touring around Mt Warning, reflecting on it, photographing, and videoing it, and staying in a caravan/trailer park on its plain, all was to culminate in a nighttime oneness with GOD event. This Revelation moment is indelibly etched on my whole being.

I had the most remarkable opportunity to experience GOD's Word firsthand, literally. I had taken leave to recuperate from illness and stayed for a few days in a caravan in my wife's original hometown. The campsite I chose significantly had a view of Mt Warning in the background. I had viewed a 'mountain' thousands of times, mainly since I was 18, and met my future wife and local farming family. Mt Warning is an imposing 'mountain' feature in the far north of New South Wales, Australia. I say mountain; in reality, it isn't in any comparative height sense like Europe/Asia or the Americas. For the oldest continent on Earth, Australia, it is quite imposing. Being a volcanic core, it stands out literally within the caldera features of a vast ancient volcano. The shape is very appealing and attractive. Its centrality within the region causes it to be a feature admired from all directions.

Over three days, I drove the 72km around its base and up to the walkers' departure point (on bitumen and gravel roads). Around sugar cane farms and through national parks and small villages, I videoed and photographed it from all possible directions, sat and reflected with it, observed it, drove and walked to crucial observation points, visited its base, and became very familiar with it. You could almost say I became one with it.

On the third day, I was awoken at night. I was very aware of my breathing and of breathing cold, fresh, clean air. I just lay there breathing deeply in through the nose, holding each breath for a couple of seconds and slowly blowing it out through the mouth. There was a real sense of presence. I started to realise it was quite a cold night and that I was relatively lying at the foot of Mt Warning. I began to get this powerful awareness that I was one with the mountain. The mountain and I had grown together significantly these past three days, and now we were at a climax. The Truth would become apparent.

I then started to get a message to write down what I was about to receive. And to be very accurate.

I soon realised that, just as in ancient times, the mountain was a conduit to GOD. Prophets from many religions had climbed mountains closer to GOD and received GOD's message for that time and place in history and often for subsequent eras. I was not to climb the mountain tonight. (Or ever again due to an injury.) But I was to climb it figuratively.

Or was it a case of GOD coming down from the mountain?

Remarkably, what followed blew me away! Without thinking about what I was to write, I found myself writing down a list of instructions, teachings, and refreshers. Was it indeed from GOD? It sure felt like it. But how could I tell? I was told within my mind not to overthink this, to go with the flow - that it was all legitimate and would become apparent as the night went on. The challenge for me was that since my 25th birthday religious experience, tears were a sign of GOD's presence; the more significant the tears, the greater the divine presence. (See 'Tears from GOD', the following article)

Yet, there were no tears tonight. But there was ecstasy and a realisation of what was happening. A font of wisdom was unfolding, and I was so, fortunately, a part of it. The list was completed. An explanation from me of what had occurred was recorded after the list. (See 'Revelation Notes' after the 'GOD's 12 Revelations' section.) And a perfect sleep followed.

The following day was a Sunday, and I attended the Catholic sacrament/ritual of the Eucharist in the church in which Karen and I were married forty years ago this year! The mass was by coincidence a First Communion Mass for the local Catholic school. During the Mass, I asked GOD if what happened last night was real – what followed was an outpouring of tears. The answer was an emphatic, "Yes!"

I then started to get a message to write down what I was about to receive…

I soon began to realise that, just as in ancient times, the mountain was a conduit

to and from

God.

'Tears from God' – One of GOD's Signs of Wisdom showing 'His' Divine Presence

My 'Road to Emmaus' experience, my epiphany, the 'Commitment to God' Day on my 25th birthday highlighted something extraordinary from God.

It became evident that when God wanted me to know something exceptional was coming from God, there would be passing on the 'Tears from God'. These are not God's tears physically, but these are tears from God spiritually, which I experience physically, emotionally, and spiritually.

There is an overwhelming sense of God's Love and Presence being intimately experienced at that moment. Words cannot describe what is happening, as it is evident to the recipient that it is on another level beyond the physical. Tears pour out in free flow. There is no everyday contorted facial expressions or sobbing, as is typically associated with crying. It isn't crying as we know it, but tears are flowing uncontrollably.

Many others also experience these Tears from God. No religion can claim this existence solely, as it occurs across several religions. This section mainly looks at the place of the Tears in Christianity, Islam, and Hinduism.

Just as these Tears overwhelmed me all those years ago, each time God needs me to realise that something extra special is happening, or that differentiation is necessary between the things of this world and the things God wants me to know about or do, or that I need strong support as part of God's plan, God shares the Tears.

Many will say that this is just emotion and that the tears come because I am emotional about something. Early on, this was my thought too. However, over time, there has developed an evident appreciation of the difference between normal emotional tears and those Tears from God.

The difference is difficult to explain, other than to say that the recipient gets this inherent feeling simultaneously as the Tears that God is making it known that God is uniquely present at that moment. It is not just like *feeling* God's presence but *knowing* God is present.

Sometimes you almost hear words from God, but you know these are your words being inspired by God. Many people would appreciate this from their own prayer life when messages come to them from God. It is God's inspiration but through your thoughtful words.

These Tears from God were called on several times as I went through these books' development. I needed to be continually reminded that the Revelations and inspired messages of the books were correct. In *1God.world: One God for All* it was especially needed for the central premise and Revelation being unconditionally accepted before it was published: that there is only one God for all religions, peoples, and cultures - forever. As well, all the inspired messages within the book up until the Mt Warning Revelation experience had been discerned as correct over several decades, yet reassurance through the Tears from God was still needed before publication. Similar support and verification from God were required for the following books, *Where's GOD: Revelations Today (2018), Jesus and Mahomad are God (2020),* and *Love is the Meaning of Life: GOD's Love* (2021) with the publication of the Revelations and inspired messages contained within.

With the initial planning done in May 2016 for the first book, it was time to get God's approval. I stood with my wife, Karen, in our kitchen one evening and let her know I wasn't sure of the central premise for publication being singled out and emphasised, as I hadn't had any confirmation message from God. I was concerned that I might have been over-stepping the mark. At that moment, a rush of tears filled my eyes – Tears from God answered my call! The message from God was palpable - that it was correct and to go ahead, write the book, and publish.

Since that time, there have been various other occasions when this assurance has been given, especially at Mt Warning. One example evolved into a video of this topic recorded with Mt Warning as a background. **

I realise many people will challenge my belief in this. However, all I can say is that I inherently know it is correct and that I have God's support and encouragement to state this publicly and emphatically.

Let us consider where the Tears from God historically come from when viewed in the three example religions of Christianity, Islam, and Hinduism.

Christianity has long believed in this phenomenon, often referred to as the 'Gift of Tears' from the Holy Spirit (God). The Holy Spirit freely gives charismatic gifts. Ewing beautifully encapsulates the closeness with God caused by these tears when she highlights how the Holy Spirit is infused into the receiver's soul. The tears' action is the physical sign and personal experience bringing about such a result. The person will often be unable to explain what has happened - that the experience is somewhat subconscious and in a different realm.

Fenelon states how Pope Francis refers to these as 'the Gift of Tears'. He emphasises how this helps prepare the receiver to see Jesus (God) and how the concept is based on the 'Spiritual Exercises' of St Ignatius, especially where Ignatius is overwhelmed by the consolation of God. The Tears are coming from a sense of deep intimacy with God, primarily while Ignatius celebrated the Eucharist in all its beauty and presence of God's love. She goes on to share theologian Tim Muldoon's thoughts on how the pope sees this as a mystical experience of a deep, preconscious conviction of God's presence. It results from an overwhelming experience of receiving God's intimate love, which can only be expressed through the free-flowing tears.

Fr Bartunek, an evangelical Christian and is now a Catholic priest, explains that this gift can occur singularly or on multiple occasions. He states that it does not mean the receiver is any holier or closer to God than others. He says it is an event to encourage those receiving or witnessing it to be in more significant and more substantial relationships with God. It provides excellent comfort from God or confirms decisions they had previously made and defence against temptation.

Physiologically, Bartunek notes how these Tears from God are not like healthy tears, resulting in sobbing due to everyday life's emotions. Still, these tears flow abundantly and freely without any physical tension or facial contortions. He also mentions that this gift isn't in scripture or the Catechism but has been referred to by various spiritual writers since the early Church.

In Al-Islam, examples of Tears from God are seen in both the Qur'an and traditions. Some examples in the Qur'an include when Tears occur as a sign of perceiving the realities of God or as a sign of wisdom. Prophets shed tears for Allah when hearing of communications from God. Tears are seen as so significant in Islamic tradition that they are a gift to humanity, to illuminate and soften the heart and bring about a great reward from God, including extinguishing God's wrath.

Rattner speaks of what he calls the emotion of devotion, a crying for God, which he explores from the Hindu and Christian traditions. Like the Christian and Islamic examples above, the Tears come from God at those special and often unique transformational moments with God. These were regular and spontaneous, purifying him to experience higher conscious states, leading to continual spiritual development.

(See 'Tears from God...' video at - https://www.youtube.com/watch?v=z5mmNvIKko4...t)

Peacefulness with GOD – a deeply personal experience

Early this year (April 2021), I headed for the Murwillumbah Showgrounds after packing up the caravan at the Chinderah caravan park, Tweed Heads, where I had stayed for a few nights to work on the last book I was up to, Book 7.

As I began the drive from the campsite, I experienced an immense feeling of enormous peacefulness, Love and tranquillity. It was a calmness of exceptional Love. This I cannot recall happening at a similar level since my 25th birthday experience. I had peaceful and Loving incidents when GOD gave me the 21 Revelations in 2016 and 2018. But these were somewhat different.

So, my trip this morning was incredibly peaceful and quiet, with a tremendous feeling of Love – Perfect Love from GOD. As I moved through this experience while driving from caravan park to showgrounds, the feeling became incredibly unique and outstanding. It was a most pleasurable, peaceful, forgiving one. So much so that I seriously considered having a forgiving, reconciliation time directly with GOD. I therefore did.

It was so powerful that I wondered where it would take me. Now I feel like it may be how you feel when going back home to GOD (Heaven). It was so Loving and 'calling' that I seriously thought of the major conclusion to whom this may introduce me while driving along the highway. However, this was not to be so. I am still here and still working for GOD. That serious and authentic Loving feeling I received from GOD earlier this year now continues with me. I just Love it!!!

That serious and
authentic Loving
feeling I received
from GOD earlier
this year

now continues with
me.

I just Love it!!!

So hopefully you will
too!!!

We need to be
genuinely open to
GOD in everything
we do.

GOD's Powerful Signs and Coincidences

Coincidences??? (See Book 4 in *the 'GOD Today' Series,* i.e., *Where's GOD? Revelations Today Photobook Companion: GOD Signs,* for explanations of spectacularly unique, exceptional, and challenging photographic examples of GOD's signs and coincidences, I was extremely fortunate to receive. It is my favourite book in this *Series,* with some out of this world photographic images.)

The showground is where you can see Mt Warning in a not far distance. These showgrounds are on the plains of the Mt Warning/Wollumbin, northern rivers of NSW, Australia. It was here that I received the first 15 of the 21 Revelations in 2016. I was on the same camping showground site when this article was originally written, in 2021, as I was in 2016.

Some coincidences based on the number 25 with spiritual overtones follow. Once these coincidences are experienced and acknowledged as reality, one method allows all folk to have or finally accept similar experiences. Why? Does it sound too outright to say that if I, as an ordinary man, can receive these, why can't others? I passionately believe that they can. This is how God often works. Those who are open to assisting GOD as disciples/followers or who will become this way over time will most likely have an opportunity to do so at some stage in their lives.

The coincidences were:

1. On arrival at the showgrounds, I was offered and accepted **site 25** from the park's manager. Coincidence? The number 25 has had significance for me ever since my 25ᵗʰ birthday. Coincidence or Gift

from GOD? This site was where I received the Revelations from GOD #1 to #15 of the 21 in 2016.

2. On my **25ᵗʰ birthday** in 1982, several coincidental events occurred on one day. The most significant was when I first received the **'Tears from God'** while being prayed over by the secondary school's principal, Sr Ann, at Seton College's 'Commitment to God' day. I also had minimal tears from GOD during my school days, when I was considering entering the priesthood, from years 10 and 11.

3. It was the exact day I **left the first secondary school** in which I taught.

4. This required moving my family, Karen, my wife, and our first daughter, aged four months, **to Tara** in southern country Queensland. **They left the previous day, while I left late that birthday afternoon.**

5. It was on the College's unique **'Commitment to GOD' Day.** Seton College is the only school that celebrated this, of that I am aware. Sr Ann was a charismatic healer, as were another six out of the fourteen teachers on staff. The day commenced with a Eucharistic Liturgy (Mass), celebrated by a charismatic priest from Melbourne, Victoria.

The rest of the day was turned over to the opportunity for students and staff to freely commit to GOD in a unique and public way if they so desired. This may have occurred anytime throughout the day. Students were free to roam throughout the campus, except those around or close to the church needed to respect the quietness – which they did brilliantly. (More details on this 25th birthday story from Seton College may be found previously on p249 in this Book 8.)

6. **Sr Ann prayed over me** after I eventually '**Let Go and Let GOD**' occurred. Until that moment, I was fighting its possibility. There was much to doubt, especially after various television shows were viewed on its healing activities from other countries over several years. The shows seemed way too unreal and quite disingenuous, at times, for many of us. The fundamentalist approach (belief in the Bible literally) seems too un-Australian for most. It isn't easy to get a handle on it. (As an example, most Australians would happily be contextual, i.e., understanding and appreciating the Bible in its most profound sense. Interpreting the Bible contextually and figuratively from the circumstances of the authors' days.)

There was quite a physical reaction from Sr Ann's laying on hands after offering me the opportunity to receive GOD exceptionally. It was so real. Getting a handle on it is now complete. I fully believe now that GOD does come to people in extraordinary ways. As she placed her hands on the top of my head, immediately **an incredible warmth appeared inside me and travelled from head to feet**. Extraordinarily **serene and peaceful** was the occasion. Quite quickly, I started to cry, **Tears from GOD**. These were not normal emotional, sobbing tears but unique God-given signs and experiences. GOD came to me specially and remarkably.

7. This was my last day at Seton College. I had resigned from the College to move to **Tara, as their Catholic primary / elementary school principal.**

I left Seton College that day surrounded by a sense of absolute Love of GOD and GOD's creations, human and other life forms. Along with an experience that had already changed my life. I Love GOD so much now that I have not had any negative thoughts about GOD or GOD's ways and expectations since that unique, extra special DAY – my 25th birthday, 39 years ago.

I left Seton College that day surrounded by a sense of absolute Love of GOD and GOD's creations, human and other life forms.

Along with an experience that had already changed my life.

I Love GOD so much now.

I have not had any negative thoughts about GOD or GOD's ways and expectations since that unique, extra special DAY –

my 25th birthday, 39 years ago.

Discerned Truths by the Author from God

At Pet's Death – Deep Love Discovered

All from my family's most Loving Cat.

Watching my family cat (14 years old) these past few weeks has led to much anxiety and sadness, as she appears to be moving towards death. She has lost an enormous amount of weight, is slow-moving, mainly interested in drinking water only and a little food and meowing quietly. She lies down for most of the day, lately in her spot where she lays during a BBQ preparation.

She very much enjoys us patting, stroking, and talking to her. This is so difficult to do and watch, considering. Yet, I know in my heart of hearts that she will be going home to God shortly.

This is what is meant by Soul=Life. The soul of my cat will be moving on, hopefully to Heaven with God (and not Hell). We will all meet up again somehow(?) in the future. This fauna and flora belief is a challenging new belief, which God has asked me to share. It has also been discerned over several years. Knowing this takes away so much of our pain.

(See also p.329ff for detail)

Highlighted Wisdom Quotes from Books One to Six - an Overview

* There is only One God for all religions, all cultures, for all time, forever.

* Jesus and **Mahomad are both Incarnations of God who lived fully as humans before becoming God in Heaven. (Revelation #15, 2016)

* Christian and Islamic leaders, theologians, and other scholars are called upon to explain #15 Revelation and how it applies to their religions and today's world.

* Islam must reject violence, especially regarding the teachings about Mahomad's lifestyle and link to today's world.

* Tears from God, Revelations from God, Incarnations of God, etc., are essential background for the book's thesis and author articles.

* Islam and the secular world need new 'Reformations' and 'Renaissances' like the historical ones, due to corrections required worldwide. A world that is seemingly moving away from God.

* 21 Revelations to the author from God in 2016 and 2018 need implementing.

* Forgiveness is crucial for a loving world, loving countries, communities, families, and individuals.

* Prophets are genuine and need to be a part of our world. God works through prophets to highlight various Revelations. Find and support today's prophets.

* We NEED God so much today. Be open to God and God's ways. God is absolute Love, loving absolutely.

* Be aware of signs and coincidences from God. Examples of signs for this author are – sun rays, sun arrows, sun flares, double rainbows, and a colossal sun cross. The author believes

these occur from God to encourage people to check and follow God's Revelations and messages, etc., as the Truth.

* Book 4 in the 'GOD Today' Series is a photobook of these signs from God. Some unique and challenging images indeed.

* The gifts of science and technologies are from God to us. This helps explain the physical world, which should then help us all to use this knowledge from God for God's things for the world.

* God revealed 'Himself' to the author and gave humanity 21 Revelations today.

* Mt Warning and its closeness to God for the author and his wife. It was on the plains of Mt Warning that God revealed the 21 Revelations for today's world.

* God loves each of us equally and absolutely and requires us to love God absolutely in return.

* Each day is a special gift from God of life. We live on a knife's edge and could live or die anytime, anywhere; this is God's choice.

*Why do we hang onto life so strongly when the possibility of being with God and living in perfection is what follows most people's lives here?

* Evil is real. Evil is when we freely decide to do, say, etc., against God.

* People have one last chance to turn back to God on their deathbed. At that instance of death, God gives us one last chance to reject evil and love God.

* Evil people who cannot change their ways and desire to enjoy evil over good/God will end up in total isolation forever – in Hell!

* We need to share our God stories. People's closeness with God depends on sharing with others and receiving these in return. The author's 26 stories in Book 1 (examples from over

his lifetime) help set the parameters for each of us to see what our stories teach us about God, Love, forgiveness, etc. We should share our stories.

* Free Will – we all have this. We need to take this a step further and use it with our informed conscience to work out what God wants from and for us.

* Gifted, talented and fortunate people owe the world.

* Share the bounty. God requires each of us to do what we can for the poor, disabled, ill, disadvantaged, etc., people of our world. Greed is evil! Sharing legitimately is needed by all.

* All people on this earth can lead rewarding, fulfilled, loving lives if only the rich could share. Even those not wealthy but with more than needed are required to share. This is our only outcome when we know that God loves us all equally.

* Humans, animals, and plants all have a 'soul'. Soul=life. Along with a relationship with GOD and each other. (Discerned)

* Love and forgiveness are essential for authentic Love.

* Love is social justice for all.

* Humans feel the same inherently, until…

* GOD is Absolute Love

* We NEED GOD

* GOD makes life so much better when we allow this to occur

* Prayer is essential communication with GOD

* People desire to live a whole life so strongly. Then die to be with GOD.

* GOD can be found in relevant music and books

* Secularism is dangerous, hollow, and leading humanity to a catastrophe. A secular Reformation is also needed today.

* Media is relatively quiet on GOD. This must change quickly.

* Evil people must stop bullying and rejecting GOD and GOD's followers

* Former Muslim Ayaan Hirsi Ali, in her book, 'Heretic', 2015, calls on everyone to make Islam go through a Reformation, as most of the world has already done historically.
* Following GOD enriches humanity
* 'Tears from GOD' occur when someone is very close to GOD.
* Teachers and parents need passion and commitments to help adolescents grow towards GOD.
* Exemplify prayer for others. Show engagement with GOD.

** The spelling of 'Mahomad' by GOD in Revelation #15, plus once as 'Mahommad' when revealed to the author by God.

Introduction to *Series* Content

The following section is presented as an opportunity for the reader interested in other topics within this Series. It is included so that the reader may become mindful of what issues and what the quantity of these topics in each book will be, for the previous Books One to Seven.

It helps with a quick overall viewing for each of these Seven books and will allow the reader to ascertain if any other books may be of interest once Book Eight has been read and reflected upon.

This Book 8 from the *'GOD Today' Series* is one of nine books written by the author, Bryan Foster. The *Series* has been developed over six years (2016-2022). Book Nine is also out in 2022. Because of the relatively high amount of time devoted to writing these books, various amounts of content appear across the nine books. Some crucial topics will appear more than once, but each time will have a different focal point or critical theme.

Also, there is a developing video series as part of this *Series*. It is called *'God Today'* and contains 30+ free (for now) videos for this theme. It is an integral part of the author's YouTube channel titled - *efozz1*. You will notice that there are over 780 videos on this channel. These have been developed over the past decade-plus and cover the author's three main themes: 1. *God Today*; 2. *Caravanning for Beginners*; 3. *Places to Stay and Things to See and Do Throughout Australia*. All from our personal experiences while travelling for themes 2 and 3. There are also other videos of interest to me on various topics. A couple of my pastimes are videography and photography.

Book 1 in '*GOD Today*' Series
'*1GOD.world: One GOD for ALL*'

CONTENTS

Some Positive Shared Messages

Bryan Foster

Background Stories by Author

Bryan Foster

Love is the Meaning of Life (2nd ed)

Book 3 in 'GOD Today' Series

'Where's GOD? Revelations Today'

CONTENTS

PART 1

GOD'S REVELATION

PART 2 UNDERSTANDING GOD

Love is the Meaning of Life (2nd ed)

Bryan Foster

Book 4 in '*GOD Today*' Series

'Where's GOD? Revelations Today Photobook Companion: GOD Signs (2nd ed).'

So much can be gained through these most incredible, spectacular images formed by God!!!

Outstanding and Unique sun, moon and cloud images, mainly with the author receiving sun arrows, etc. Confused?

These need to be seen to be believed!

Author's Favourite Photobook and Book.

Introduction

Foreword

Unique Sun Formations

Easter Sun Crosses

Sun Arrows and Flares

Love is the Meaning of Life (2nd ed)

Bryan Foster

Book 5 in *'GOD Today' Series*

Jesus and Mahomad are GOD*

Love is the Meaning of Life (2nd ed)

Introduction   46

Author

Truths

Bryan Foster

Jesus and Mahomad* are GOD

ONE GOD - TWO INCARNATIONS

(*NB. The spelling of 'Mahomad' is deliberate. It is as told by GOD to the author.)

21 REVELATIONS FOR TODAY

Renumbering Revelations   **154**

Bryan Foster

Book 6 in '*GOD Today*' Series

Love is the Meaning of Life: GOD's Love

CONTENTS

What is LOVE? Some everyday examples…

Love is the Meaning of Life (2nd ed)

LOVE IS THE MEANING OF LIFE:

GOD'S LOVE

Absolute LOVE of GOD

GOD and Prayer

Bryan Foster

GOD, Us and LOVE

GOD's LOVE

Love is the Meaning of Life (2nd ed)

Where is GOD's Love?

RELIGIOUS CHALLENGES TODAY

LOVE'S Challenges for GOD's People

Bryan Foster

RELIGIOUS SOLUTIONS TODAY

GOD's Special Loving Gifts for Us

Some Loving Challenges

Love is the Meaning of Life (2nd ed)

Reformations Needed Today?

GOD, Teachers and Adolescents

Bryan Foster

Author's 42 years Teacher Background

Book 7 of the *God Today' Series*
Wisdom: God's Hints and Tips
CONTENTS

GOD's HINTS and TIPS

Introduction to Wisdom Quotes   49

Bryan Foster

Key MESSAGES in the '*GOD Today*' *Series* (2016-2021) to the Author - Revelations and Discerned Messages from GOD

Wisdom Quotes in Grey Boxes - Revelations from GOD to Bryan or Discerned by Bryan from GOD. From the *'GOD Today' Series*. Book by Book.

Appendices

These appendices assist with the background of **GOD's** Revelations and Inspired Messages and Bryan's pronouncement of these for **GOD** to today's world. The following appendices are aimed at those seeking more detail or a refresher from what has come before in this *Series* since Book 1 in 2016.

Bryan Foster

304

Each book in this '*GOD Today*' *Series*

invites us in various ways to join in the discovery of GOD,

GOD's Wisdom and Revelations, Inspired Messages and Love,

as we journey towards our own personal and communal salvation with GOD on Earth, and if so blessed, later in Heaven.

Heaven is the culmination for those who have Loved GOD and others intensely over their lives

(Allowing for times of human weakness and lack of forgiveness, though).

And at the time of death

make this final decision to be with GOD forever...

We must eventually accept that this relationship with GOD is the most positive, enhancing, honest, forgiving, and absolutely loving one we could ever imagine.

The closer we get to the Absolutely Loving GOD of Wisdom, the sooner we can find out about our true soulful selves and our place in GOD's plans.

We find out that GOD's divine relationship with us all is so much more significant and impressive than for one we could ever imagine.

Warning!

Too many people have this incorrect appreciation of Good and Bad and its various outcomes.

Following God is good.

Following Evil is terribly bad.

People who think ignoring God's guidance and commands, by doing whatever they feel like,

no matter how stupid,

hurtful to self and others, and wrong, etc,

is all in the name of fun -

and somehow good for them,

are absolutely wrong?!

Tears from God

There is an overwhelming sense of God's love and presence being intimately experienced at that moment of receiving the Tears from God.

Words cannot describe what is happening… it is on another level beyond the physical.

It is not crying or sobbing as we know it, but tears incredibly, lovingly, flowing uncontrollably -

Loving Tears from the Loving God.

Conclusion Book 8B (Selections & Author Articles)

Love is the Meaning of Life could develop into *Love is the Meaning of Life: GOD's Love* - if we so choose. i.e., bring God more into the challenges. But how? The critical difference, you will have noticed, is that 'God' appears in Book 8B's title but not in Book A's title. The inclusion of God into 8B depths the quality and quantity of the Love, taking it to the Absolute top level of God's Divine Love for each of us and each living creation - be these animals, plants, or the top of the scale of creations - the human animals.

We can undoubtedly exhibit and live a somewhat loving life without God, but it would be on a much lesser level. We need to ask God for Loving assistance regularly. This is a challenge for the secular world. These people mostly know no other way of Loving; hence God doesn't exist in their daily lives. (Maybe there are other times throughout their lives when God does play a part, either consciously or subconsciously?)

When people face enormous challenges within their daily lives, they usually call on God for assistance, whether this is a regular occurrence or not, and whether it is from their secular mind responses or others', e.g., God. One of the most common responses people carry within our world today is the incredible overuse of the phrase, "Oh my God!" It reads well here, yet once heard allowed, there comes the realisation that it isn't mostly asking for God's help, but just an exclamation response with little or no request from God for anything.

All people need considerable Love in their lives. This Love helps to bring empathy, forgiveness, truth, lack of greed, etc. It helps with so much of today's lifestyles – with or without God. Having general Love is good. Having God's Love is absolutely top level.

God=Absolute Love

This is the Love God will share equally

with all people.

This Love comes directly from God.

It is up to us to accept this offer

or reject this offer!

Bibliography

Book 8A. (8B=Summaries & Articles from Book 6)

Primary Source

GOD - Revelations and Inspired Messages Given to the Author

Secondary Sources

Books

Ayaan, Ali, '*Heretic: Why Islam Needs a Reformation Now*', 2015

Fishman, R., *No Man's Land*, 2014, Rising Tide Books, Sydney.

Foster, B., *1God.world: One God for All*, 2016, Great Development Publishers, Gold Coast.

Foster, B., *Mt Warning God's Revelations: Photobook Companion to 1God.world*, 2017, Great Development Publishers, Gold Coast.

Foster, B., *Where's God? Revelations Today*, 2018, Great Development Publishers, Gold Coast.

Foster, B., *Where's God? Revelations Today Photobook Companion: GOD Signs*, 2018, Great Development Publishers, Gold Coast.

Tragic Face of Teenage Despair in *The Australian*, 21/3/19, NewsCorp, p.1.

Websites – Book 8A plus 8B Selections

2016 Census QuickStats: Tennant Creek
http://www.censusdata.abs.gov.au/census_services/getprod
uct/census/2016/quickstat/SSC70251

http://www.abc.net.au/…/same-sex-marriage-survey-
ca…/8958176

ABS
http://www.censusdata.abs.gov.au/census_services/getprod
uct/census/2016/quickstat/SSC70251

Ali, Ayaan Hirsi, '*Heretic: Why Islam Needs a Reformation Now*',
2015, https://www.goodreads.com/book/show/18669183-
heretic

Ayaan's Wikipedia biography (seems quite accurate from my
readings) https://en.wikipedia.org/wiki/Ayaan_Hirsi_Ali

https://www.amazon.com/BryanFoster/e/B005DOPRMO/
ref=sr_tc_2_0?qid=1514764108&sr=1-2-ent

Bryan Foster Author https://www.bryanfosterauthor.com/

Bryan Foster's YouTube channel (efozz1) - 780+ travel and
'How to caravan/trailer for beginners by Fozzie' videos, etc.,
at https://www.youtube.com/user/efozz1

Catalyst 2017 Series 18: ABC iview

Catholic Social Teaching for Best Practice
https://www.caritas.org.au/learn/schools/just-visiting/cst-
for-best-practice

Love is the Meaning of Life (2nd ed)

Census 2016: what's changed for Indigenous Australians? https://theconversation.com/census-2016-whats-changed-for-indigenous-australians-79836

http://www.censusdata.abs.gov.au/census_services/getprod uct/census/2016/quickstat/SSC70251

Christine Roberts' (1967) song: http://splash.abc.net.au/home#!/media/104826/?id=10482 6

Close the Gap Report on *The Drum* 2/03/19 https://www.abc.net.au/news/2019-03-21/the-drum-thursday-march-21/10927204

http://www.dorotheamackellar.com.au/archive/mycountry.h tm

'GOD Today' Series https://www.godtodayseries.com/where-s-god

God Today Series on *Facebook* https://www.facebook.com/groups/389602698051426/

Heartbeat: The Miracle Inside You, Dr Nikki Stamp, 2017 Series 18, http://iview.abc.net.au/programs/catalyst/SC1602H005S00

Leonard Cohen's 'Hallelujah' at https://www.youtube.com/watch?v=YrLk4vdY28Q

http://leodowney.com/discography/leo-downey-2008/ http://leodowney.com/about-leo/

Leo Downey. https://www.youtube.com/watch?v=UCdA2UN5KqA

Leo Downey, http://leodowney.com/discography/leo-downey-2008/

Leo Downey's *'The Rest of My Life'* – at https://www.youtube.com/watch?v=dS-OblC7c9M

Madeline, an 18-year-old from Canberra, http://www.theaustralian.com.au/…/9fb76f1b9f080a729aed ccb42…

'My Country' poem: http://www.dorotheamackellar.com.au/archive/mycountry.h tmhttp://www.dorotheamackellar.com.au/

Photobook Series by Bryan Foster and Karen Foster http://au.blurb.com/user/efozz1?profile_preview=true

Russell Drysdale art examples: https://www.artgallery.nsw.gov.au/collection/works/?artist_ id=drysdale-russell

Social Justice 10 Principles, University of St Thomas, (2010): Layout 1 (stthomas.edu)

Social Teaching for Best Practice https://www.caritas.org.au/learn/schools/just-visiting/cst-for-best-practice

'Tears from God…' https://www.youtube.com/watch?v=z5mmNvIKko4…t

Tennant Creek - Drive Through video by Bryan Foster: https://www.youtube.com/watch?v=PNsop7an73I

Tennant Creek Aboriginal leaders say $80 million aid package prompted by toddler's rape being misdirected - ABC News

The Origins of Social Justice…

Love is the Meaning of Life (2nd ed)

https://isi.org/intercollegiate-review/the-origins-of-social-justice-taparelli-dazeglio/

These Indigenous doctors are on a mission to help their communities thrive, not just survive - ABC News (2019)

The Origins of Social Justice…
https://isi.org/intercollegiate-review/the-origins-of-social-justice-taparelli-dazeglio/

Wujal Wujal township
http://www.wujalwujalcouncil.qld.gov.au/

What are human rights
https://www.humanrights.gov.au/about/what-are-human-rights

(All websites viewed 2021/2, unless otherwise stated.)

Index

'GOD Today' Series by Author, Bryan Foster - Book Summaries (2016-2022)

Book 1. *1GOD.world: One GOD for All (Author Articles)* introduced in detail the first major Revelation from GOD today and challenged the reader to search and find GOD through other people, nature, and GOD's Revelations and inspired messages. It introduced the reader to the One and Only God of all time, for all religions, cultures and countries. This Book 1 shared twenty-six of the author's personal, spiritual, finding-GOD, 'everyday' stories, hopefully encouraging and assisting others in seeking and finding GOD. A series of inspired messages discerned by the author over his lifetime were shared and published in 2016. **OUT NOW**

Book 2. *Mt Warning GOD's Revelation: Photobook Companion to '1GOD.world'* is a 72-kilometre photographic exploration around Mt Warning and up to the walking track's starting point. These were taken over three years, culminating with the Revelations from GOD on the plains at the foot of the mountain one cold winter's night. It is a photographic and written story of the spectacular and spiritually inspiring Mt Warning and its surrounding towns, landscapes, and fauna. Images are taken from most angles around its 72km base plus the road up to the walking track. Book 2 was published in 2017. **OUT NOW**

Book 3. *Where's GOD? Revelations Today (Author Articles)* invites the reader to continue the journey of exploring who and where GOD is for them and what are

GOD's messages for today's world. It details the twelve Revelations from GOD for today introduced in the previous two books. A collection of another six inspired messages received within that same 24-hour Revelation period is shared. A key focus is on assisting the reader in their appreciation, understanding, and searches for GOD in today's world. **OUT NOW**

Book 4. *Where's GOD? Revelations Today Photobook Companion: GOD Signs* surprises the reader with some exceptionally spectacular and unique photographic images, possibly formed from various reflections and refractions of the Sun or most likely given directly from GOD. Some sun arrows and sun flares formed across the author, along with spectacular sunshine shapes created in the sky. Especially look in the images presented for sun-formed arrows, flares, huge Easter sun cross, double rainbows, and cloud formations. These occurred at venues on the plains of, and at the foot of, Mt Warning, Cabarita and Kingscliff beaches, Straddie, at Cylinder Beach, North Stradbroke Island, and inland at Texas on the Queensland/New South Wales border, along with Vernon in B.C., Canada. The Sun is central for many people to imagine and discern GOD and GOD's beyond-our-reality's extraordinary powers. Other spectacular sunrise and sunset images are shared. Our Sun is the centre of our world – no sun, no lives. ** The photos are so genuinely striking and unique that Book 4 is the author's favourite Book.** These pictures say thousands of words combined. ****Author's Favourite – unique, spectacular photos***** It was published in 2018. **OUT NOW**

Book 5. *Jesus and *Mahomad are GOD (Author Articles)* (Revelation #15) was released in July 2020. A massive challenge for around fifty per cent of the world's population is issued. Both Jesus and Mahomad are the incarnate One and Only GOD. Part of Revelation #15 is this Book's title. Prayer and relationships with GOD and the incarnate GOD hold critical possibilities for our future world. The first and possibly overawing Revelation that is the basis for this Book came during the Revelations from GOD to the author in May 2016. The world will be religiously challenged like possibly no other time in history. The extremists and the violent must remain faithful and peaceful, no matter their likely strong desire to do otherwise. No excuse! Our loving, most peaceful GOD allows for nothing else. GOD won't accept any violence, especially in 'His' name! One essential outcome becomes the divine example of GOD's Love – we are all equal and holy before GOD until we sin. Forgiveness from us is then required. The most profound and exemplary reality of GOD is the Incarnations of Jesus and Mahomad at different times in history. (*Mahomad mostly spelt this way by God when giving the 2016 Revelations to the author.) **OUT NOW**

Book 6. *Love is The Meaning of Life: GOD'S Love (Author Articles) (1st ed.)* was released in early 2021. A significant exploration of what Love is and how it affects us all introduces this Book and is the theme followed throughout. There is a substantial discussion on the types of Love, its positive and sometimes negative impacts, and how we can grow in true Love throughout our lifetimes with our unique loved ones, family, friends, colleagues, communities, and of course, with GOD. GOD is seen as the Absolute Lover in its perfect sense. Who loves us all equally and desires our perfect union on this Earth and ultimately with GOD in Heaven.

GOD's Love and people's Love are explored in detail.
OUT NOW

Book 7. Wisdom: GOD's Hints and Tips (Author Articles)

Most readers should see a book of Wisdom from GOD to the author as something special for humankind to see. GOD is sharing some outstanding essential beliefs and lifestyle messages. So many Revelations, Inspired Messages, and Vital Loving information from GOD to today's people are shared. This book was released in 2021. It is a unique encounter with some refreshingly insightful quotes, including challenging ones. The first group of extracts from the three collections, i.e. Revelations, will, similarly to the author, range across the reader's lifetime and are linked as examples to that mentioned stage of life. The bulk comes from the first 60 years of a person's life. How these can help each of us, no matter our age or maturity, will be the reader's challenge and need some genuine support as we all progress through life. People who especially enjoy spiritual and human reflections will be drawn to many quotes. The second group is the 21 Revelations to the author in 2016 and 2018. At the same time, the third group contains the highlighted Inspired GODly Messages found in each book within this *Series*. Each one encourages serious reflection and addition to our lexicon. The author developed these with GOD's perfect influence and written over the past 40 years. These should add and support each reader's quotes from God. Then shared with others as felt appropriate.
OUT NOW

Book 8 *(8A Book plus 8B Selections from Book 6)* create *Love is The Meaning of Life (Author Articles) (2ⁿᵈ ed)* (2022). This second edition of the *Love is The Meaning of Life: God's Love (1st ed.)* book does not reflect a considerable emphasis on GOD in the first section, i.e. 8A, as written in 2018. Book 8A is followed with Part 8B with Selections from Book 6. This book has some special topics linked to book 8A and the Selections from Book 6 in Part 8B. The language and discussions will be clear and non-complex, hopefully without the often-found necessity by various writers to make it so convoluted. Doing so often leads to losing the level of appreciation by the reader of the essential topic of Love. Yet, because GOD is the perfect Love and needed for any deep loving relationship, there is a limited but necessary discussion on this point in the Selections written in Part 8B, i.e., the last 1/3 of the book. The author can never minimise GOD's Truth in any edition of these books. An accurate story/explanation of what Love is and its impact on our lives is explored. People often get confused when speaking of Love, as there are several types and levels of Love, which impact us all to various degrees. GOD is Absolute Love. Love is what we are trying to gain continually throughout our lives! Circumstance's change, and so do relationships. When we achieve this Love, we also gain God! It will be a book on Love for all people. Maybe you could keep an open mind and see where this may lead you, with or without your belief in God, over as many years as you would like to consider and reflect on it. **OUT NOW**

Book 9. *Love is The Meaning of Life GOD's Love: Photobook* **Companion (2022)** will actively support two of the previous textbooks, Book 6 and Book 8, through significant photographic images. Some beautiful and authentic photos of our Love and our lives on this Earth and the surrounding cosmos are the basis of this photobook. The images will sometimes be quite challenging. These should support each reader as they discover various divine and life messages and support from GOD. Combined with multiple literary genres used to enhance or support the photos, this Book 9 will be strong encouragement for those wishing for more Love in their lives and the world. Its emphasis is on how GOD, being Absolute Love, can help the reader develop their GOD/Love relationships mainly through the presentation of many, what could also be considered somewhat challenging images. **OUT 2022**

All people need considerable Love in their lives.

This Love helps to bring empathy, forgiveness, truth, lack of greed, etc.

It helps with so much of today's lifestyles – with or without God.

Having general Love is good.

Yet, having God's Love is absolutely top level.

God=Absolute Love for all people!!!

Include God in your daily lives!!!

Ask God as simply as you need to,

"Please help me God, with whatever I need to bring me closer and closer to your Love over my lifetime…"

The 13 Significant Revelations (R) and Inspired Messages (IM) from GOD in this *Series* are:

1. R. 21+1 Revelations from GOD to the author in May 1982 (1 Revelation) (while teaching at Seton College). And May 2016 (15 Revelations) and Nov. 2018 (6 Revelations) while caravan camping on the plains of Mt Warning, NSW, Australia.

2. R. There is ONLY ONE GOD for all people, religions, and cultures, forever.

3. R. Jesus and Mohamad are both GOD – Incarnations of GOD (i.e., GOD became human at two times in history, of which we are now aware).

4. R. GOD uses signs and symbols to attract us and help us progress positively to Salvation. Various photographic signs the author received since 2018 are – the large Easter SUN Cross in the sky near Texas, Queensland on the NSW side of the border; SUN flares, sun arrows, sunrays going across me, at heart and brain angles, from the sun sparkling through the rainforest canopy. Along with an arrow going over a published book in this Series that I handheld. All at various treed locations: SUN rays from a small cloud moving out sideways and vertically above Mt Warning/Wollumbin. Along with a double rainbow somewhat above my caravan at Amity Point, Straddie, North Stradbroke Island. (See Book 4 for some spectacularly unique images from GOD – you will be much more than just pleasantly surprised. These may even seem to be impossible. But are not!)

(***Book 4 is the author's favourite in this Series. Be Truly Amazed!!! Spectacular images from God and stories to share are shown throughout this photobook. ***)

5. R. GOD Loves all People Equally. People move away from GOD, not GOD moving away from us.

6. R. GOD confirmed that the 'Tears from GOD' received by people are one of GOD's physical signs to support the divine Truth or essential information for humanity.

7. R. We NEED to NEED GOD and be vulnerable to GOD out of the deepest of respect and admittance of the Absolute GODly power over creation and life, being from the one and only Creator, Perfection, and Powerful well beyond our human understanding. We acknowledge GOD's LOVE and place as being so outside what we could ever imagine but being Absolute Love for each of us. The invitation for each of us is to agree and respond positively every day to our NEEDS through GOD being essential. Don't ignore God or God's possibilities. Show the NEED you have. Absolute respect for God shows our Love and Need for God the divine, one and only, forever!

8. R. The world needs to acknowledge that modern-day prophets are needed and are here worldwide. Could people we know be one? Possibly but as yet, this is unknown? + Other prophets worldwide, maybe?

9. IM. All living people, flora, and fauna have the opportunity to be with GOD after our deaths, as discerned by this book's author over many years. All have souls. This is a significant difference from the norm that will challenge various religions. Each religion needs to be asked to explain

this new original belief received by the author over many years to their followers over time. SOULS=LIFE

10. IM   Science is GOD's gift to humanity. It needs to be used to discover how everything within our world works. Then, use the information to develop ways and means of making this world a better place for all people.

11. IM.   GOD's Love is the Meaning of Life. Continually ask God for this Love over your lifetime. Show genuine gratitude and thank God whenever this love is shared with you and others!

12. IM. In general, does the western world need another Reformation and/or Renaissance for its generally unholy, secular emphasis? Is GOD missing way too much in the critical world and of life and earthly decisions? Is the western world turning away from GOD substantially? We NEED GOD like never before!

13. IM.   Aayan Ali's strong proposition for Islam to have its own Reformation and/or Renaissance similar to the western world's historical challenges and responses is very much needed for world peace and for literally far less violence. See Ali's 2015 book, '*Heretic: Why Islam Needs a Reformation Now*'. Ali moved from Somalia to Saudi Arabia with her family, then escaped to the Netherlands and became a politician. This was followed by her move to the USA and Harvard University, where she excelled, receiving significant awards and academic roles.

Deep Love is Truly Discovered Through the Death of a Family Pet - Details

Our 14-year-old cat, Bella, was diagnosed with fluid in her lungs and, according to the vet, was past living a decent quality of life. We decided, along with the vet, that we should bring her life to an end. Karen and I stayed and assisted with the process. Those who have experienced this event with any pet know the heart-wrenching sorrow and pain involved, as is most people's loss of animal life. For me, Bella's transition to Heaven was a similar effect, but as significant in the emotions brought out for my dad's death three years ago. The similarity is that each of Dad's and Bella's deaths occurred over three weeks and that the incredible Love of Dad and Bella was incredibly similar. Hence little time to prepare for both deaths. Just as for Bella, I had to sign the permission to administer higher-order drugs for my dad's pain. Our cat, Bella, received various medications from the vet for her euthanasia. It was the level of sadness for our Bella, which I felt so strongly recently.

So sad, but also glad that we did. Even while she waited, Bella snuggled in a towel held by Karen. She was awake and looked so beautiful and at peace as if she knew. Even large dogs barking and growling in the next room through the closed door did not affect her. Did she actually know? We said our farewells. This was when that incredible loving moment began to hit me just before she died. The vet lady said a line, which virtually meant she was going to God. The vet said, "She is now passing on." Even though I am pretty sure her idea of 'passing on' wasn't what mine was, she was most likely indirectly somewhat of my belief, maybe? It was so lovely to hear either way.

I felt so much love from Bella, Karen next to me, and the young lady vet. I prayed for Bella just audibly that she would be returning home to God right now, and along with Karen, we said that we'd see her there sometime in the future! Then off she went. I then gave her a big hug.

It was 18 years ago since our previous experience of this, when our cat, Kelly, was also put down due to age and associated illnesses. At that time, I held Kelly, as Karen did with Bella. Our youngest, nine-year-old daughter was also there - a most difficult time for us.

Most powerfully, at that moment of death, I felt Kelly's last breath go and found myself taking a quick sharp breath in virtual shock, I think! I simultaneously felt that most extremely loving experience for the first time. It was as if I was breathing in some of her lifeforce before her soul=lifeforce returned to God in Heaven. While I lived at home until I was 17 and in a different world to now, e.g., there were mostly no fences, but the pet animals wandered the neighbourhood. All my previous pets mainly died from being hit by a vehicle or other injury or illness. Our parents protected us from any vision of their death moments or bodily remains.

Bella was my book writing companion for the last 2.5 years since I retired from teaching and started writing books full-time in this *'GOD Today' Series*. She is already incredibly missed, which fills us with sadness, yet we celebrate her transition from Earth to God!

Out of this whole, yet relatively short, event, something has lit a fire in both Karen's and my hearts and souls. In the last couple of years, I have discerned from GOD that all living creations, fauna, flora and humanity, have a soul and an excellent opportunity to be welcomed by God to Heaven at their death. How this occurs is still very much a mystery from God. God has many mysteries attached to us, life and death, and who or what can make it to salvation at death, etc. It is a challenging, discerned belief. It has much to do with God being a mystery. Not a physical entity but divinely so powerful and loving that any comprehension we imagine we have must be so lacking. Our religions need to take these new beliefs on board and help their congregations know and appreciate them, as these come from God to His people through the author.

This was explained in Book 6, the 1ˢᵗ edition of this Book 8, *Love is the Meaning of Life: God's Love, (1ˢᵗ ed), (Author Articles),* 2021.

Beyond the difficulty, i.e., comprehending the soul and its placement in all living creations, comes something outstandingly brilliant and spectacular. Combining Bella, the cat's soul, and Karen's and my souls, something 'magical' (not magic though) and depth defying LOVE had been experienced yesterday, during Bella's transition/passing to God's Heaven.

The most authentic, powerful, brilliant example of Love I have ever experienced occurred. The Tears from God were on another extremely high level. Words definitely cannot express this most dynamic and robust feeling of genuine, real LOVE! Watching the peaceful and quiet Bella wrapped up in a towel and held by Karen, waiting for what would happen to unfold. **There was this most incredibly high emotion never felt by us before. That is the RUSH of LOVE from GOD that occurred to Karen and me.** I don't believe it was 'Tears from God' previously discussed in this Series and now regularly experienced by both of us. It was different but similar in some ways? It just seemed so much more, not as experienced before, but completely overtaking our appreciation of what we thought Love truly is! After 43 years of marriage, you'd think that we'd be calling from the hilltops about our experience of Love so far. But this experience seemed to go well beyond that level of Love. In reality, probably not, but it did seem that way at that particularly significant moment!

Beyond that, it is impossible to describe the experience of this AWESOME Loving feeling from GOD, being just before and after Bella's death.

It seemed to be better understood when comparing some of our human and lifestyle LOVE experiences, e.g., births, weddings, major life successes, and discovering God in our lives. Etc. Yet, it was even better than these, mostly.

A little test: Place in your mind the feelings you got when observing a young, very much loving couple being married; being at the birth of a child; watching a champion athlete win one of the competitions, almost impossible to do events; **discovering God within your life and wanting and needing that extraordinary love we all can experience when we're ready, and God is ready to accommodate us with all our quirks and bad decisions, greed and lacking forgiveness, etc**.

We can't force the God experience/closeness, but we need to be prepared for when it comes.

Because God is Absolute Love, we tried to imagine what God 'feels' during the examples above, if God 'feels' anything at all emotionally, etc.? Or maybe because God is God, there most likely would-be other functions, behaviours, 'feelings', totally unbeknown to us non-divine humans. There is a good possibility that this knowledge will happen at our deaths if we make it to Heaven. **We must believe and live, God=Absolute Love!** We could then say how incredible must Heaven be if the Love God gave us that afternoon at the animal refuge was even just a minute example for the remainder of our hoped-for eternity in Heaven.

We experienced something so minor to God's True LOVE when God came to us there. Yet, it was so beyond our human understanding that it became somewhat apparent what God is like and how unique and Loving and brilliant it will be when we reach Heaven at our deaths.

Once people experience this level of Godly Love, they would lack any serious judgment and intelligence if they chose badness, being deliberately wrong, rejecting God outright, and being evil as their lifestyle choices.

God=Absolute Love!

We truly must believe and live it.

We could then say how incredible must Heaven be, if the Love God gave us both that afternoon at the animal refuge was even just a minute example for the remainder of our hoped-for eternity in Heaven.

… it became somewhat apparent [at Bella's last moments and death] what God is like and how unique and absolutely Loving it will be, when we reach Heaven at our deaths.

Author's Photobooks

'My Australia Photobooks' Series – 12 x photobooks of Northern Territory and (FNQ) Far North Queensland, (2014-5)

Mt Warning Wollumbin Circuit: a Photographic Journey, (2018)

'Straddie' *North Stradbroke Island: Photobook of Natural & Shared Beauty*, (2019)

Other Textbooks by Bryan Foster

Marketing Schools and Churches

School Marketing Manual for the Digital Age (3ʳᵈ ed), (2008-1ˢᵗ, 2009-2ⁿᵈ, 2011-3ʳᵈ)

Church Marketing Manual for the Digital Age (2ⁿᵈ ed), (2009-1ˢᵗ, 2011-2ⁿᵈ)

Author's Websites

For further information and reader response:

https://www.bryanfosterauthor.com/ (Author's website)

https://www.godtodayseries.com/ (Main website for this *Series*. Includes the blog commenced in 2016)

http://www.greatdevelopmentspublishers.com/ Publisher's new webpage. (Original website started in 2007, closed 12/2018. Now a new webpage)

https://www.facebook.com/groups/389602698051 426/ (God Today - Facebook)

https://au.linkedin.com/in/bryanfoster (LinkedIn)

https://www.youtube.com/user/efozz1 - (780+ YouTube videos commenced in 2009 and covered various themes, e.g., God Today; Marketing Schools and churches; and many hints, tips, and places to stay for Caravan Beginners.)

https://twitter.com/1Godworld1 (Twitter being developed)

https://www.instagram.com/(Instagram)(1godworld being developed)

'GOD Today' Series by Bryan Foster

Books 1-9 + Video Series. 2016-2022.

Book 1. *1GOD.world: One GOD for All, (Author Articles)* (2016)

Book 2. *Mt Warning GOD's Revelation: Photobook Companion to '1GOD.world'*, (2017)

Book 3. *Where's GOD? Revelations Today, (Author Articles)* (2018)

Book 4. *Where's GOD? Revelations Today Photobook Companion: GOD Signs (2ⁿᵈed)* (2018) ** Author's favourite** - Images So Unique and God-Given!

Video Series. *Where's GOD? Revelations Today,* YouTube (efozz1 or CaravanAus channels n) (2018)

Book 5. *Jesus and Mahomad are GOD (Author Articles)* (2020)

Book 6. *Love is the Meaning of Life: GOD'S Love (1ˢᵗed) (Author Articles)* (2021)

Book 7. *Wisdom: GOD's Hints and Tips (Author Articles)* (2021)

Book 8. *(8A and B). Love is the Meaning of Life (2ⁿᵈed) (Author Articles)* (2022)

Book 9. *Love is the Meaning of Life GOD'S Love: Photobook Companion* (Draft stage) (2022)

SUMMARY

The 13 Significant Revelations (R) and Inspired Messages (IM) from GOD in this *Series* are:

1. 21+1 Revelations from God to Author – 1982, 2016, 2018. (Books 1,3,5,6,7,8.)
2. Only 1 God forever for all religions and all people. (Books 1, 3)
3. Jesus and Mahomad are both God Incarnate. (Book 5)
4. God uses signs and symbols, e.g., giant Easter sun cross in the sky over Texas, NSW. (It is Book 4's cover image.) Sun arrows, sun rays, etc. (Books 3,4.)
5. 'Tears from God' are another of the signs from God to support 'His' divine truth with us. (Books 1,3,5,6,7,8.)
6. God Loves all people equally. People choose to move away from God, i.e., how sinning occurs. (Books 1,3,7)
7. We need to need God and be vulnerable to God out of the Absolute Love of God. Place God as #1 above everyone and everything else. (Books 3,5)
8. Prophets are needed worldwide. Specially to pass on God's Revelations and Inspired Messages to all people worldwide. (Books 5,7)

9. All living people, fauna, and flora have the possibility to go to Heaven at death. All have souls. Life=Soul. Choose God above all else at death. Choosing evil will cause a creation's ending to be Hell. (Books 6,7)

10. Science is God's gift to humanity. Through discovering how things work on earth and in the cosmos, we can use this information to make our world a better and more just place for all. Science cannot prove or disprove the existence of God. God is divine; Science is physical. (Books 1,3)

11. God's Love is the Meaning of Life. (See Books 6,8.)

12. Is the western world turning away from GOD substantially? We NEED GOD like never before! (Books 3,5)

13. Islam needs its Reformation and Renaissance, like the historical western world's experiences, according to former refugee and asylum seeker Aayan Ali, from her 2015 book *Heretic: Why Islam Needs a Reformation Now*. (Books 3,5,6)

Great Developments Pty Ltd

trading as

Great Development Publishers

Gold Coast, Queensland, Australia.

Bryan Foster and Karen Foster

Directors.

bryanwfoster@gmail.com

https://www.bryanfosterauthor.com

https://www.godtodayseries.com

Facebook QR Code – GOD Today

GREAT
DEVELOPMENTS

Publishers